THE COMPLETE LLC

GUIDE FOR BEGINNERS

SIMPLE STEPS TO FORM YOUR ENTITY,

MANAGE YOUR ASSETS, AND MAXIMIZE TAX

BENEFITS FOR YOUR GROWING BUSINESS

***

T.J. GRIFFIN

© **Copyright T.J. Griffin, 2024 - All rights reserved.**

The content within this book may not be reproduced, duplicated or transmitted without direct written permission from the author or the publisher.

Under no circumstances will any blame or legal responsibility be held against the publisher, or author, for any damages, reparation, or monetary loss due to the information contained within this book. Either directly or indirectly. You are responsible for your own choices, actions, and results.

Legal Notice:

This book is copyright protected. This book is only for personal use. You cannot amend, distribute, sell, use, quote or paraphrase any part, of the content within this book, without the consent of the author or publisher.

Disclaimer Notice:

Please note the information contained within this document is for educational and entertainment purposes only. All effort has been expended to present accurate, up-to-date, and reliable, complete information. No warranties of any kind are declared or implied. Readers acknowledge that the author is not engaging in the rendering of legal, financial, medical or professional advice. The content within this book has been derived from various sources. Please consult a licensed professional before attempting any techniques outlined in this book.

By reading this document, the reader agrees that under no circumstances is the author responsible for any losses, direct or indirect, which are incurred as a result of the use of the information contained within this document, including, but not limited to, — errors, omissions, or inaccuracies.

TABLE OF CONTENTS

Introduction — 9

1. **LAYING THE FOUNDATION: UNDERSTANDING LLC BASICS** — 11
   - 1.1 What is an LLC? A Simple Explanation for Beginners — 12
   - 1.2 Comparing Business Structures: Why Choose an LLC Over Others? — 14
   - 1.3 The Legal Benefits of Forming an LLC: Asset Protection Explained — 16
   - 1.4 Understanding LLC Pass-Through Taxation: What It Means for You — 18

2. **THE INITIAL STEPS TO LLC FORMATION** — 21
   - 2.1 Choosing a Legal and Effective Name for Your LLC — 21
   - 2.2 Filing Your Articles of Organization: A Step-by-Step Guide — 24
   - 2.3 The Importance of an Operating Agreement: Key Inclusions — 26
   - 2.4 Obtaining an EIN and Why It Matters for Your LLC — 29

3. **FINANCIAL MANAGEMENT FOR LLCS** — 33
   - 3.1 Setting Up Your LLC's Bank Accounts: Best Practices — 33
   - 3.2 Accounting Basics for LLC Owners: Keeping Your Finances in Check — 36
   - 3.3 Exploring the Tax Obligations and Benefits for LLCs — 38
   - 3.4 Applying for Business Credit: A Guide for LLCs — 42

4. **NAVIGATING STATE-SPECIFIC LLC REGULATIONS** — 45
   - 4.1 Understanding and Navigating Your State's LLC Regulations — 45
   - 4.2 Multi-State Operations: Managing LLC Compliance Across Borders — 47
   - 4.3 The Impact of Local Laws on Your LLC Operations — 50
   - 4.4 Case Study: Successfully Setting Up an LLC in California vs. New York — 52

5. PROTECTING YOUR ASSETS — 55
- 5.1 Asset Protection Strategies for LLC Owners — 55
- 5.2 The Role of Insurance in Protecting Your LLC — 58
- 5.3 Separating Personal and Business Finances: How and Why — 60
- 5.4 Investing in Your Future: Personal Finance for LLC Owners — 62
- 5.5 Legal Safeguards to Enhance Your LLC's Asset Protection — 65

6. DAILY OPERATIONS AND MANAGEMENT — 69
- 6.1 Effective Daily Management Practices for Your LLC — 69
- 6.2 Hiring Employees vs. Contractors: What LLCs Need to Know — 72
- 6.3 Implementing Standard Operating Procedures (SOPs) in Your LLC — 74
- 6.4 Crisis Management: Keeping Your LLC Stable in Tough Times — 76

7. GROWTH STRATEGIES FOR LLCS — 83
- 7.1 Organic Growth Strategies for Small LLCs — 83
- 7.2 Exploring Mergers and Acquisitions: Is It Right for Your LLC? — 86
- 7.3 Innovative Marketing Strategies for LLC Expansion — 87
- 7.4 Utilizing Technology for Business Growth — 88

8. COMPLIANCE AND LEGAL ISSUES — 93
- 8.1 Annual Filings and Compliance Checklists for LLCs — 93
- 8.2 Handling Legal Disputes: Tips for LLC Owners — 95
- 8.3 Updating Your LLC Documentation: When and How — 97
- 8.4 The Consequences of Non-Compliance for LLCs — 99

9. FINANCING YOUR LLC — 103
- 9.1 Bootstrapping Your LLC: Strategies for Self-Funding — 103
- 9.2 Securing Loans and Lines of Credit: A Guide for LLCs — 106
- 9.3 Attracting Investors: Pitching Your LLC Successfully — 108
- 9.4 Crowdfunding Opportunities for LLCs: A Modern Approach to Funding — 110
- Engaging With Backers: The Heart of Crowdfunding — 111

10. ADVANCED TAX STRATEGIES — 113
    10.1 Advanced Tax Deductions and Credits for LLCs — 113
    10.2 Handling Multi-State Taxation for Expanding LLCs — 115
    10.3 Tax Planning: Preparing for Year-End Tax Obligations — 118
    10.4 Leveraging Tax Professionals: When You Should Hire an Expert — 120

11. ADAPTING TO CHANGES AND FUTURE-PROOFING YOUR LLC — 123
    11.1 Anticipating Market Trends: How to Keep Your LLC Competitive — 123
    11.2 The Impact of Technological Advances on Your LLC — 125
    11.3 Legislative Changes: Staying Informed and Compliant — 127
    11.4 Succession Planning: Preparing your LLC for future — 130

12. REAL-WORLD INSIGHTS AND CASE STUDIES — 133
    12.1 Case Study: Successful Asset Protection Through an LLC — 134
    12.2 From Startup to Success: An LLC Growth Story — 136
    12.3 Overcoming Compliance Challenges: Lessons from an LLC Owner — 138
    12.4 Innovative Financing: How an LLC Secured Non-Traditional Funding — 140

    Conclusion — 145
    Glossary of Terms — 147
    References — 151

A Special Gift For You!! 👋

Start Your Journey with Confidence!

https://thecornerpage.myflodesk.com/starterkit

The Complete LLC Guide For Beginners

Understanding LLC Basics

* * *

T.J. Griffin

INTRODUCTION

Recently, there has been a noticeable boom in entrepreneurship. More individuals than ever are stepping into business ownership, looking for financial independence and the thrill of creating something valuable. Last year alone, people registered over 2 million new businesses in the United States, with a significant portion choosing the Limited Liability Company (LLC) structure. Why? Because LLCs offer a blend of flexibility and protection that is hard to beat. LLC is more than just timely information; it is critical if you are considering joining the ranks of self-starters and innovators.

Establishing my own LLC presented numerous challenges, but I learned valuable lessons I am eager to share with you. I aim to transform complex legal and business concepts into explicit, actionable knowledge you can easily apply.

This book guides you through the entire process of forming and nurturing your LLC. It outlines everything from initial setup to strategies for growth and compliance in a way that's easy to follow and understand.

We'll cover various topics, from the basics of LLC formation to advanced strategies for sustaining and growing your business. This book is designed for emerging entrepreneurs and small business owners considering converting to an LLC. The insights and strategies provided will be valuable tools to help you achieve financial independence and master the world of LLCs, paving the way for lifelong success.

1

LAYING THE FOUNDATION: UNDERSTANDING LLC BASICS

S tarting an LLC can be overwhelming, especially if you're new. By aiming and simplifying the process, you will understand why an LLC might be the perfect setup for your business dreams. We'll explain what an LLC is, why it could fit your needs, and how to avoid common pitfalls many new entrepreneurs face. You will see how forming an LLC can provide a solid foundation for your business, saving you from future headaches and setting you up for success.

1.1 WHAT IS AN LLC? A SIMPLE EXPLANATION FOR BEGINNERS

Definition and Structure

Many entrepreneurs choose to form an LLC, with over 2 million LLCs created in the United States each year. This popularity stems from the LLC's unique benefits, such as limited liability protection, tax flexibility, and minimal compliance requirements. Let's see why this business form is attractive to so many businesses.

An LLC, or Limited Liability Company, is a flexible and valuable business structure. It combines the tax benefits of a partnership or sole proprietorship with the liability protection of a corporation, allowing you to include profits and losses in your income without facing the typically higher corporate tax rates.

At the same time, you have protection from personal liability for business debts and claims, unlike in standard partnerships or sole proprietorships.

Formation Process

Setting up an LLC involves several essential steps. First, you need a **business name** that is unique and compliant with state regulations, typically including 'LLC' or 'Limited Company' at the end. For example, if you want to name your bakery "Sweet Treats," it should be registered as "Sweet Treats LLC" or "Sweet Treats Limited Company. Next, you file the **"Articles of Organization"** with your state's business filing office. This document is essential for officially creating your LLC. In Kansas, for example, you would file Form DL-51, the

Articles of Organization, with the Kansas Secretary of State. If you have to file in Texas, you would file Form 205, Certificate of Formation, with the Texas Secretary of State. Each state has its form, called the **Articles of Organization**. You'll also need an **Operating Agreement** outlining your LLC's ownership structure and procedures. Even if it's not required in every state, having an Operating Agreement can prevent future disagreements or confusion among members.

Additionally, some states have specific requirements for LLCs. For example, you must publish a notice about your new LLC in New York in two newspapers. In California, you must periodically file a 'Statement of Information' instead of a publication requirement to confirm your LLC's status with the state.

Benefits for Small Business Owners

Why do small business owners give LLCs two thumbs up? For starters, they're straightforward to set up and don't need you to jump through as many hoops as corporations. They offer flexibility in management and aren't picky about the number of owners—or members, as we call them. An LLC is a flexible option, whether it's just you or you and several partners.

Most business owners like the liability protection of an LLC. It means you can take business risks without risking your assets—like your house or savings. And remember the tax benefits. LLCs, unlike corporations, aren't taxed as separate business entities. Instead, all the profits and losses pass through to the owners' income, avoiding double taxation. Sweet deal, right?

Common Misconceptions

There are a few misconceptions we have to address. First off, while LLCs are great for asset protection, they don't make you invincible. If you guarantee a business loan or engage in illegal activities, your LLC won't shield you from liability. Also, LLCs are not a one-size-fits-all solution. They work wonders for many small businesses, but depending on your industry or long-term goals, another business structure, like a corporation, might be a better fit. It's all about finding the proper structure for your business. Choosing the right structure is crucial, affecting everything from your day-to-day operations to your peace of mind as a business owner. Take your time, weigh your options, and ensure we build this LLC correctly from the ground up. Let's set the foundation for long-term success.

1.2 COMPARING BUSINESS STRUCTURES: WHY CHOOSE AN LLC OVER OTHERS?

When deciding on a business structure, it's essential to consider your options. A corporation provides strong protection but is complex to manage, while a sole proprietorship is simple but offers less protection. An LLC combines both benefits, providing the flexibility of a sole proprietorship with the legal protection of a corporation, making it a practical choice for many small business owners.

Comparison with Sole Proprietorships and Partnerships

Sole proprietorships and partnerships are easy to set up and manage but have significant risks. Under a sole proprietorship, if your business faces financial trouble or a lawsuit, your assets, such as your house or savings, are at risk. Creditors can pursue your personal property to settle business debts.

An LLC offers 'limited liability protection,' meaning your assets are better protected if something goes wrong with your business. This protection allows you to focus on running your business without worrying about losing your assets due to business issues.

Advantages over Corporations

Another comparison is that of an LLC's advantage over a corporation. While corporations can raise more capital, they are also more complex to manage and come with significant paperwork and regulatory requirements. Corporations must hold regular board meetings, maintain detailed records, and file extensive documentation. Additionally, corporations often face double taxation—paying taxes at the corporate level and on shareholders' income.

In contrast, LLCs offer a more straightforward structure with fewer compliance requirements, making them an attractive option for small business owners seeking protection without the administrative burden. LLCs also benefit from pass-through taxation, meaning the business itself isn't taxed—only the income that passes through to your taxes, providing a tax-efficient way to manage your business income.

Situational Examples

Imagine you're running a small artisan coffee shop. As a sole proprietor, the simplicity is excellent. Still, losing your savings if the business doesn't perform is like a constant espresso shot of anxiety. Switch that scenario to an LLC. Now, you have better protection for your assets from business liabilities. You can focus on perfecting your cold brew instead of sweating over losing your nest egg. Or you're an app developer with a nifty new product. As a corporation, you might attract more investors. Still, the rigidity of operations and the double tax hit could crimp your style (and profits). An LLC could give you the necessary flexibility to innovate while keeping things streamlined and your tax situation more favorable.

Visual Aids

To help you visualize the differences, here's a handy chart comparing key features, benefits, and drawbacks of these business structures:

Feature	Sole Proprietorship	Partnership	LLC	Corporation
Personal Liability	Unlimited	Unlimited	Limited	Limited
Taxation	Pass-through	Pass-through	Pass-through optional	Double Taxation
Formal Requirements	Minimal	Minimal	Moderate	High
Flexibility in Management	High	Moderate	High	Low
Setup Complexity	Low	Low	Moderate	High

This chart illustrates why an LLC is the right choice if you value flexibility, protection, and more straightforward tax arrangements without sacrificing the potential for growth and adaptability.

It is an attractive option for many entrepreneurs, whether you're just starting or looking to restructure. Considering an LLC could be a pivotal decision in shaping the future of your business.

1.3 THE LEGAL BENEFITS OF FORMING AN LLC: ASSET PROTECTION EXPLAINED

One key advantage of forming an LLC is the limited liability it offers. This feature protects your assets from business debts and legal issues. When you operate as an LLC, the company becomes its legal entity. If your business faces financial trouble or lawsuits, your assets, such as your home, car, and personal savings, are generally protected from creditors and legal claims. This separation provides peace of mind, knowing that your personal life remains secure from business risks.

Real-World Example

You are a successful coffee shop owner. One day, despite regular maintenance, your espresso machine malfunctions, and a customer gets injured. A lawsuit against an LLC would target your business assets, not your assets. This protection ensures that your savings, retirement funds, and other personal assets remain untouched.

However, there are situations where this protection only partially applies. For instance, if you guarantee a business loan, your assets could be at risk if your business fails to repay the loan. Additionally, engaging in fraudulent activities or unethical business practices can lead to a court "piercing the corporate veil," removing your personal liability protection.

Strengthening Your LLC's Protection

To enhance your LLC's protection, follow these best practices:

1. **Separate Finances**: Maintain distinct personal and business bank accounts to avoid commingling funds.
2. **Compliance**: Ensure your business follows all necessary regulations and maintains proper records.
3. **Insurance**: Obtain appropriate insurance policies, such as liability, property, and professional insurance, to cover potential gaps in protection. For example, professional liability insurance can protect your consulting firm from lawsuits related to advice provided to clients.

By combining the legal structure of an LLC with diligent management and adequate insurance coverage, you create a strong defense around your assets. This approach not only safeguards your finances but also supports the growth and stability of your business. Ensuring that your entrepreneurial efforts do not jeopardize your assets is crucial for long-term success and peace of mind.

1.4 UNDERSTANDING LLC PASS-THROUGH TAXATION: WHAT IT MEANS FOR YOU

If you've ever played a board game that involves fake money, you know the thrill of banking that big win without any real-world tax implications. Would it be sweet if real life worked more like that? If you're running an LLC, pass-through taxation provides this benefit. It's not your average tax loophole; it's an entirely legal way to manage business profits that can save you from the headache of corporate double taxation—that dreaded scenario where your money gets taxed twice, first as corporate income and then as personal income when you pull it out as dividends.

With pass-through taxation, your LLC's profits and losses travel directly to your tax return, bypassing the corporate tax level entirely. It's like having a direct line from your business to your pocket, only stopping briefly at the IRS for a quick check-in. This setup is a big win for LLC members because it simplifies the tax process tremendously. You report the business's financial outcomes on your tax forms using Schedule C, part of your tax return, and complete the process quickly.

This superpower of pass-through taxation isn't just about making tax time less of a chore; it also offers some nifty flexibility in how you can be taxed. Typically, by default, an LLC is treated as a disregarded entity if there's just one member or a partnership if there are more. However, you can tailor things by taxing your LLC as an S corporation.

Why might you consider this? While the LLC's default tax status works great for many, choosing the S corp election can benefit significantly when your business rakes in more cash than you need to cover your living expenses.

Opting for S corporation tax treatment allows you to pay yourself a reasonable salary for your work and distribute any profits over that as dividends. The kicker? Those dividends aren't subject to self-employment taxes covering Social Security and Medicare. This exemption can lead to substantial tax savings, particularly if you're in a higher income bracket–you get functionality plus a bit of extra room to keep more of what you earn.

Let's break this down with a real-world example.

A freelance graphic designer set up an LLC for his business. Last year, he pulled in $120,000. As a sole proprietor, all that income would be subject to self-employment taxes, which can be like running a marathon—exhausting and not something you look forward to. But if he chooses S corporation tax treatment, he could pay himself a reasonable salary, such as $70,000, which feels fair. He could take the remaining $50,000 as dividends, avoiding the self-employment tax. His wallet will thank him at the end of that tax marathon.

But before you change your LLC's tax classification, putting on your strategist hat is crucial. Switching to an S corporation might save you money on taxes, but it also comes with more stringent rules and the need for consistent payroll management. The best choice varies based on your situation, financial goals, and how much paperwork you can handle before you start feeling like you're drowning in a sea of forms.

Here are some actionable tax planning tips for those wondering how to make this work. First, consult with a knowledgeable tax advisor who understands your business. This advisor will help you navigate the tax landscape, discuss the optimal times to switch your tax status, and determine a reasonable salary for your industry. Planning is essential, so consider setting up quarterly tax check-ins to ensure everything runs smoothly and prevent tax issues.

Pass-through taxation is not just a feature of your business structure; it is a powerful tool that can significantly benefit your personal and business financial situation with the proper knowledge and planning. By making the tax laws work for you, you can maximize your financial efficiency and focus on growing your business without losing money to unnecessary taxes.

The Complete LLC Guide For Beginners

Step-By-Step Formation

* * *

T.J. Griffin

2

THE INITIAL STEPS TO LLC FORMATION

Starting an LLC is like building your dream home, but instead of bricks and mortar, you're using legal documents and tax forms. The first step is choosing a name for your LLC. While it may seem simple, the task involves more than just coming up with something catchy. The name you choose is crucial for your business identity and legal compliance. Plus, it can be difficult to change later, so getting it right from the start is essential. Here's how to pick a legally compliant name for marketing.

2.1 CHOOSING A LEGAL AND EFFECTIVE NAME FOR YOUR LLC

Legal Requirements

Every state in the United States requires that your LLC's name ends with an LLC identifier, such as "LLC" or "Limited Liability Company." The identifier indicates to anyone doing business with you that they are dealing with an LLC and not another type of business structure. It helps set expectations about your company's liability arrangements and structure.

Another legal detail to keep in mind is avoiding names that could confuse your LLC with a government agency (think "FBI Artworks LLC" or "U.S. Treasury Studio"). Using such names is a big no-no and can lead to a bureaucratic headache.

Each state also has a list of restricted words that you can't use without special permissions, such as "Bank," "Attorney," or "University." Check these out on your state's Secretary of State website to stay off the naughty list.

Name Availability Check

How do you make sure the name you love is available? You don't want to set your heart on "Amazing Coffee LLC" only to find out it's already taken. Most states have an online database where you can search for business names. Here's a quick step-by-step guide on how to navigate these databases:

1. **Visit Your State's Business Filing Agency Website**: This is usually the Secretary of State's office, but it can vary.
2. **Find the Business Name Search Section**: Look for a link that says "Business Entity Search," "Business Name Availability," or something similar.
3. **Enter Your Desired Business Name:** Type in the name you're considering and follow any formatting or filtering options to refine your search.
4. **Review the Results:** You'll see a list of similar business names. If your exact name appears, that's a no-go. If it's clear, you're good to proceed.

Considerations for Branding

Choosing a legally available name is one thing; ensuring it resonates with your target audience is another. Your business name is the first handshake between you and your potential customer. It should reflect your business's identity, values, and what you offer. If you're opening a spa, "Relaxation Oasis LLC" creates a different impression than "Get Pampered Quick LLC." Think about your brand's personality and choose the name that reflects it.

SEO (Search Engine Optimization) is an essential factor to consider. Including keywords commonly used to search for services can improve your online visibility. For example, if you're a plumber in Houston, a name like "Houstonian Plumbing Solutions LLC" might be more effective online than something generic like "Fix-It-All Services LLC."

Registering a DBA

Sometimes, the name under which you register your LLC differs from the name you want for your day-to-day operations. That's where a DBA (Doing Business As) comes in handy. A DBA allows you to conduct business under a different name without forming a new LLC. For example, if "Smith Group LLC" is too formal for your funky jewelry shop, you might opt for a DBA like "Smith's Chic Boutique."

Registering a DBA involves the following steps:

- Fill out a form with your state or county.
- Paying a fee.
- Sometimes, the DBA is in a local newspaper.

It's like getting a nickname legally recognized. Plus, it allows you the flexibility to branch out or pivot without changing your formal LLC name, which can be great for testing new product lines or business ideas.

By choosing a name that's not only legally sound but also a strong representation of your brand, you lay a solid foundation for your business identity. From legal compliance to market appeal, the correct name sets the stage for everything that follows in your business adventure. So take your time, do your homework, and choose a name you'll be proud to put on business cards, websites, and maybe even t-shirts one day!

2.2 FILING YOUR ARTICLES OF ORGANIZATION: A STEP-BY-STEP GUIDE

You've chosen a great name for your LLC and are ready to make it official. Next up on your to-do list is to file your Articles of Organization. Think of this document as your LLC's birth certificate. It's the official start of your business in the eyes of the state. Without it, your LLC would be a fantastic idea floating in the entrepreneurial space.

Understanding the Document

The Articles of Organization serve as the charter for your LLC, legitimizing your business by registering it with the state. This formality initiates your legal protections and sets the stage for business operations. Typically, the information required on this form includes:

- The name of the LLC.
- Its principal place of business.
- The names and contact details of its members (you and any partners).

You'll also need to specify your registered agent—the person or company authorized to receive legal papers on behalf of your LLC. Specifying the registered agent is crucial because the state needs to know who will receive legal documents if someone sues your LLC. Filing the Articles of Organization can usually be done online, by mail, or in person, depending on your preference and your state's offer. Each method has its process, so let's break them down:

1. **Online**: This is the express lane. Most states have streamlined their systems so you can file online through the Secretary of State's website. You fill out the form, pay the fee (more on fees in a bit), and hit submit. Voilà, you're on your way to official LLC status. Often, this is the quickest method, with some states offering immediate approval.
2. **By Mail:** For those who prefer a more traditional route or enjoy the suspense of waiting, filing by mail is an option. Download the form from your state's website, fill it out, include a check for the fee, and send it to the state office. The downside is that it can take several weeks to process, depending on the backlog at your state office.
3. **In-Person:** If you like to look someone in the eye when you hand over important documents, trekking down to the state office and filing in person might be your style. It's also a good option if you're crunching on time and your state offers same-day processing for in-person filings.

Fees and Timelines

The cost of filing your Articles of Organization varies significantly, typically ranging from $50 to $500, depending on the state. Each state sets its fee schedule so that the cost can differ based on your location. Online filings are often processed immediately or within a few business days, while mail-in forms take 3 to 4 weeks. Check your state's Secretary of State website before filing for the most current fee schedule and processing times.

Common Mistakes to Avoid

Completing government forms can be challenging, and the Articles of Organization are no exception. Here are some common mistakes to avoid:

- **Typos in the LLC Name:** Make sure the name on your Articles matches what you've reserved. 'Lightning Bolt Photography LLC' differs from 'Lighting Bolt Photography LLC'. One sounds super fast; the other might be a business fixing broken lamps.
- **Incorrect Registered Agent Info:** This is not the place to fudge details. Make sure the registered agent's name and address are spot-on. If the state can't find your agent, you could miss out on crucial legal notices.
- **Leaving Sections Blank:** Fill out every applicable section. If a section doesn't apply, write 'N/A' (not applicable). Blank sections can lead to processing delays or even rejections.
- **Signature Snafus**: Remember to sign the form! An unsigned form is like a ticket without a signature—it won't get you far.

By clarifying these common mistakes and choosing the suitable filing method for your needs, you can ensure the process goes as smoothly as possible. Remember, this step is more than just paperwork; it's the legal launch of your business, providing the foundation for everything you do as an LLC. So take a deep breath, double-check everything, and prepare to step into your role as an official business owner. Your LLC isn't just an idea anymore—it's about to become a reality.

2.3 THE IMPORTANCE OF AN OPERATING AGREEMENT: KEY INCLUSIONS

Imagine you've just formed the ideal business partnership under your new LLC. The Operating Agreement acts like a manager, ensuring everyone works together smoothly. This document outlines how your

LLC operates, specifying who makes decisions and how members distribute profits. It serves as your business's rulebook, helping you avoid conflicts and work together toward success.

Purpose of an Operating Agreement

Why is this document so crucial? Beyond keeping internal harmony, the Operating Agreement sets clear expectations. It defines each member's rights and responsibilities, ensuring everyone understands their roles and expectations. Clarifying these roles is not just bureaucratic fluff; ensuring your business runs smoothly is essential. Whether it's deciding on the split of profits, managing business debts, or handling unexpected hiccups, this agreement has the answers. It's your go-to guide for navigating the internal operations of your LLC, providing a clear path forward for decision-making, conflict resolution, and day-to-day management.

Key Components

Now, what goes into this magical manuscript? Here's a breakdown of the must-haves:

1. **Distribution of Profits and Losses**: This section should answer questions like: How are profits and losses distributed among members? Is it evenly split or based on the initial investment? Clearly defining this aspect sets the financial expectations for your partnership.
2. **Management Structure**: Does your LLC have a manager, or will all members share in decision-making? Specifying this helps avoid power struggles and ensures smooth governance, whether it's a majority vote, unanimous decision, or manager's call.
3. **Procedures for Adding or Removing Members**: This section should detail how new members can join, the conditions under which members can exit, and what happens to their

shares. Having a transparent process in place ensures smooth transitions when members change.
4. **Handling of Disputes**: Your Operating Agreement should include dispute resolution procedures, such as mediation, arbitration, or other methods to handle conflicts effectively. These procedures ensure the continued smooth operation of your business.

Customization for Your LLC

While templates are a good starting point, it's essential to customize your Operating Agreement to fit your business needs. Each LLC is unique, with its own goals and requirements. By tailoring your agreement, you ensure it meets your business's needs. Customize your agreement to include details like how profits are shared, the duties of each member, and the decision-making process. Customizing your Operating Agreement makes your LLC more efficient and helps prevent misunderstandings and manage challenges effectively.

Legal Implications

Legally, the Operating Agreement is more than just an internal document. While not always required by law, it's a powerful tool in legal proceedings. It can help resolve disputes internally and in the court by providing a precise reference point to which judges and arbitrators can defer. With an operating agreement, you often rely on state default rules, which might align with your business's interests or dynamics. It's like having a customized map versus relying on vague street signs — one will get you to your destination more reliably.

By crafting a thoughtful, detailed Operating Agreement, you set your LLC up for smoother operations and more explicit directions. It's about ensuring everyone plays their part right, understands the score, and knows how to handle the solos and the rests. With this document in your band's back pocket, you're ready to take on the business world's big stage, confident that your LLC's internal dynamics won't miss a beat.

2.4 OBTAINING AN EIN AND WHY IT MATTERS FOR YOUR LLC

An Employer Identification Number (EIN) is like your LLC's social security number. It's a unique nine-digit number assigned by the IRS that you'll use more often than you think. Why bother with an EIN? With one, your LLC can legally hire employees, open business bank accounts, or pay taxes. It's essentially your LLC's ticket to entering the business world officially and legally.

What is an EIN and Why You Need It

An EIN is not just another bureaucratic hoop to jump through; it's a fundamental aspect of your business's identity. You need this number to file various tax forms, which helps shield your social security number from potentially risky exposure. Think of it as a protective barrier that separates your personal and business finances. Whether you plan to hire a team, open a business bank account, or apply for business licenses, your EIN is your LLC's identifier in all these situations. It's about as essential as coffee on a Monday morning—sure, you could get by without it, but it wouldn't be pretty.

How to Apply for an EIN

Getting an EIN is surprisingly straightforward, and best of all, it's free. You can apply for an EIN through the IRS directly, and there are a few ways to do it: online, by fax, or by mail. The online method is the quickest; you visit the IRS website, fill out the digital form, and typically receive your EIN instantly. If you're more old-school or love the feel of paper, you can fill out Form SS-4 and fax or mail it to the IRS. Just keep in mind that the processing times for fax and mail are longer—about four business days for fax and up to four weeks by mail.

When applying, you'll need to provide some basic info about your LLC, including the legal name and address and the Social Security Number (SSN), Individual Taxpayer Identification Number (ITIN), or existing EIN of the LLC's principal officer (which is likely you). It's a simple process, but ensure all your information is accurate to avoid any bureaucratic back-and-forth with the IRS.

Using Your EIN

Once you have your EIN, it's time to put it to work. This number will appear on all official documents, tax returns, and financial statements. It would be best to have it when you hire employees, as you will use it for all employment tax reports and deposits. You'll use it to set up your business bank account, which adds a layer of professionalism and helps manage your finances by keeping business and personal expenses separate. Remember, using your EIN instead of your SSN reduces the risk of identity theft, which gives you more peace of mind.

Maintaining Your EIN

Your EIN is for life—well, the life of your business, anyway. It doesn't expire, and once assigned to your LLC, it isn't reused or reissued to another company. However, if the structure or ownership of your LLC changes significantly, you might need to apply for a new EIN. For instance, a new EIN is likely necessary if you transition from a sole proprietorship to an LLC or from an LLC to a corporation. Keeping your EIN up to date ensures that all your business's activities are accurately tracked and legally compliant, keeping the IRS happy and your business running smoothly.

We've navigated through the crucial steps of forming your LLC:

- Choosing the perfect name
- Filing your Articles of Organization
- Crafting a solid Operating Agreement
- Obtaining your EIN

Each step builds on the others, forming a sturdy foundation that transforms your business from a concept into a fully operational entity. With this knowledge, you're well on your way to turning your business dreams into reality, equipped to handle the exciting challenges and opportunities in the next chapter of your entrepreneurial adventure.

The Complete LLC Guide For Beginners

Financial Management/ Asset Protection

***

T.J. Griffin

3

FINANCIAL MANAGEMENT FOR LLCS

Managing your LLC's finances is a crucial and dynamic part of your business. Setting up your LLC's bank accounts is the first order of business. This process is essential for safeguarding your funds and planning for future growth. Effective financial management will help you navigate challenges and seize opportunities as they arise.

3.1 SETTING UP YOUR LLC'S BANK ACCOUNTS: BEST PRACTICES

Choosing the Right Bank

Choosing a bank for your business is crucial. It would help to have a reliable partner who understands your needs and won't surprise you with unexpected fees. Start by listing your requirements. Do you prioritize advanced online banking capabilities because you prefer managing finances remotely? Or do you focus on low transaction fees because every penny counts when running a business? Identifying your priorities will help you find the right banking partner.

Consider banks that are friendly to small businesses. Some banks offer services tailored to the needs of small enterprises, like discounted transaction fees or specialized account managers who know what they're talking about. Don't be shy—ask other local business owners or hit online forums to get the scoop on which banks treat their business customers like rockstars.

Once you've chosen a few banks, compare their fees, services, and perks. It's like making a pros-and-cons list for potential mates. Does Bank A offer fantastic customer service but higher fees? Does Bank B give you free online transactions but have a website that looks like it's from the 90s?

Choose the bank that best balances these factors for your specific needs. Remember, the right bank will make you feel like your business's finances are in good hands—safe, understood, and well-managed.

Opening the Account

Now that you've chosen your bank, it's time to open your account officially. Opening your account is more than just a formality; it is the financial foundation of your business operations.

What do you need to take with you to your bank? You'll need your **EIN** (remember that handy number we talked about in the last chapter?), your **Articles of Organization**, and probably a **resolution** identifying authorized signers if your LLC has multiple members. Establishing the rules for who can authorize spending is similar to setting guidelines for financial control within your LLC.

Head to the bank with these documents (or use their online application if you're digitally inclined) and open that account–a big step in legitimizing your business. It separates your finances from your business dealings, which keeps the IRS happy and ensures that your assets are more likely to stay safe and sound if your company ever faces financial issues.

Banking Services for LLCs

Consider what additional banking services can make your life easier. Need to handle cash transactions? Look into merchant services. Want a safety net or plan to expand? Think about lines of credit. Are you planning on buying new equipment or a space? Business loans might be on your horizon. And let's not forget about business credit cards—they can be a fantastic tool for handling day-to-day expenses while also helping you rack up rewards or cashback. Pay that balance off monthly because high interest rates can sneak up on you like a ninja at night.

Maintaining Account Security

Last but not least, let's talk about security. Great power (in this case, access to your business funds) comes with great responsibility. Set up transaction alerts to monitor your money like a hawk. Use strong, unique passwords for any online banking portals, and consider two-factor authentication to add an extra layer of security. Regularly review your account statements to catch any unauthorized transactions because the sooner you spot something fishy, the sooner you can deal with it. Remember, keeping your business's finances secure isn't just about protecting your money but your business's future.

With your bank accounts set up and secure, you're ready to manage your finances confidently. Whether handling daily expenses or planning for growth, you've laid a solid foundation for financial success. We'll explore the basics of accounting, but for now, celebrate completing one of your LLC's first significant steps in financial management.

3.2 ACCOUNTING BASICS FOR LLC OWNERS: KEEPING YOUR FINANCES IN CHECK

You've set up your bank account and feel like a financial wizard—or at least not completely lost at sea. Now, let's chat about the backbone of your business's financial health: *accounting basics*. If the thought of dealing with numbers all day gives you high school math class flashbacks, don't worry; I will break down these concepts to make them easy to understand.

Understanding basic accounting principles is like knowing the road rules before driving. There are two main methods you might encounter: *cash and accrual accounting*. With *cash accounting*, you record transactions when cash changes hands. It's simple: Money comes in, you record it, and money goes out; you jot it down. This method is super straightforward and gives you a clear picture of how much cash you have at any given time.

On the other hand, accrual accounting is like keeping track of promises. You record income as soon as you earn it (like sending out an invoice) and expenses when you incur them (like receiving a bill), regardless of when the money plops into or flies out of your bank account.

While this method requires more mental gymnastics, it provides a more accurate picture of your business's financial health, especially if your company has many pending payments or expenses that must be addressed and settled.

A golden rule of business management to know is meticulous record-keeping. It's not just about being organized enough to find your desk under all those papers; it's about having a solid grasp of your business's financial pulse.

Good records help you forecast future cash flows, understand your business cycles, and impress potential investors with top-notch professionalism.

Tools like accounting software can be your best friend here, automating much of the grunt work and reducing human error. Whether you choose a simple app or advanced software that makes you feel like a Wall Street trader, the goal is to keep track of every penny and ensure your financial data is as tidy as a pin.

Effectively managing cash flow is akin to ensuring your garden has the right amount of water—not too dry, not flooded. You need to monitor the cash coming in and going out, ensuring that the timing of these flows keeps your business healthy. This strategy could mean delaying outflows until after your inflows are secure or finding ways to speed up receivables when anticipating a dry spell. Don't forget to plan for seasonal variations. Ensure that a predictable, slow season doesn't catch you off guard without a financial safety net.

Lastly, let's demystify the income, balance, and cash flow statements. Think of these as your business's report cards. The income statement summarizes your revenues and expenses over a period, telling you whether you operated at a profit or loss. The balance and grace of your financial ballet, if you will. The balance sheet provides a snapshot of what you own (assets), what you owe (liabilities), and what's left over for you (equity) at a specific point in time. It's like a photograph capturing a moment in your business's life, showing you the net worth of your enterprise. And the cash flow statement? Tracking the actual flow of cash in and out helps you understand the liquidity of your business. This understanding is crucial because cash is king, as any seasoned business owner will tell you.

Financial statements are crucial for understanding your business's performance.

- **Income Statement**: This summary of revenues and expenses over a period shows whether your business operated at a profit or loss.

- **Balance Sheet**: This provides a snapshot of your assets, liabilities, and equity at a specific time and shows your business's net worth.
- **Cash Flow Statement**: This tracks the actual flow of cash in and out, helping you understand your business's liquidity.

By getting familiar with these accounting principles and practices, you can crunch numbers and make informed, strategic decisions that will keep your business thriving.

With your financial foundations solid as a rock, you can focus on steering your company toward growth and success, armed with the knowledge and tools to keep your finances in check. The world of business accounting might seem vast and complex. Still, with these basics, you're well-equipped to navigate it confidently.

3.3 EXPLORING THE TAX OBLIGATIONS AND BENEFITS FOR LLCS

Taxes might not be the most exhilarating topic under the sun—navigating the labyrinth of LLC tax obligations can feel like trying to solve a Rubik's Cube blindfolded. Understanding your tax duties and benefits is essential for maximizing savings and ensuring compliance. Let's explore this critical aspect together.

First, every LLC faces a slew of tax obligations—ranging from federal to state and sometimes even local taxes. On the federal level, the IRS wants to know about your income. Because LLCs enjoy pass-through taxation, your business's income and losses pass through to your tax return.

This setup simplifies tax filing, but don't get too comfortable—each state might have specific tax rules. Some states treat LLCs like the federal government does, with pass-through taxation. In contrast, others have a franchise tax or a renewal fee, which is more like a membership fee for the privilege of doing business there.

Then there are local taxes. Depending on where your LLC operates, you might also owe local taxes. These could be business property taxes if you own your workspace or gross receipts taxes based on your total revenue. It's crucial to check with your local tax authority to see what applies to you. Think of it like checking the weather before you head out—be prepared for whatever might come your way.

How do you maximize those tax benefits? One standard deduction for LLC owners is the home office deduction. If you manage your empire from home, you can deduct some of your housing costs—mortgage interest, insurance, utilities, and repairs. The key is to use the space regularly and exclusively for your business.

Business expenses are another area where you can see some tax relief. You can write off everything from office supplies to business travel as long as it's ordinary and necessary for your business. Keep those receipts; they're your golden tickets to deductions.

Remember retirement contributions. Suppose you set up a retirement plan for yourself and your employees. In that case, you can often deduct your donations, which lowers your taxable income while you save for the future. It's like eating your cake and having it, too—saving for your golden years while trimming your tax bill today.

Handling sales tax is another beast altogether. If you sell physical products, you may need to collect sales tax. But here's the kicker: you only need to collect sales tax if your business has a nexus in your customer's state. A nexus means having a significant presence, such as an office, warehouse, or salesperson.

Once you determine where you have a nexus, you'll need to register for a sales tax permit in that state. This process can often be done online on the state's Department of Revenue website. After registering, you'll collect sales tax on all eligible sales in that state, then report and remit those taxes according to the state's deadlines. It's like being a middleman—you collect the tax from your customers and pass it to the state.

Finally, your company will have annual tax filing requirements. Your LLC might not pay taxes directly, but you must still file a yearly tax return to report your income and expenses. The specifics depend on how you form your LLC.

For example, if the IRS classifies your LLC as a disregarded entity, it treats the LLC as you for tax purposes. In that case, you'll report your LLC's income and expenses on Schedule C, part of your tax return. If your LLC has more than one member, you'll likely need to file Form 1065, an informational return for partnerships. And if you opt for S corporation status, you'll need to file Form 1120S. Each form has its own set of rules and deadlines, so mark your calendar to avoid late fees and penalties.

FINANCIAL MANAGEMENT FOR LLCS | 41

Here's a chart summarizing the due dates for federal and state tax forms:

Tax Type	Form	Federal Due Date	State Due Date
Individual Tax Returns	Form 1040	April 15 (or next business day)	Typically April 15
Extended Individual Returns	Form 1040 (extension)	October 15	Varies by state
Estimated Tax Payments		April 15, June 15, September 15, January 15	Often aligns with federal
S Corporation Returns	Form 1120-S	March 15	Typically aligns with federal
Partnership Returns	Form 1065	March 15	Typically aligns with federal
C Corporation Returns	Form 1120	April 15	Typically aligns with federal
Extended Business Returns		September 15 (S Corps & Partnerships) October 15 (C Corps)	Varies by state
Employment Tax Returns	Form 941	January 31, April 30, July 31, October 31	Typically aligns with federal
Information Returns	Form 1099	January 31 (to recipients) February 28 (to IRS, paper) March 31 (to IRS, electronic)	Typically aligns with federal
Sales Tax Returns		Not applicable	Monthly, quarterly, or annually

Notes:

- **Federal Deadlines**: If a federal due date falls on a weekend or holiday, the deadline is usually extended to the next business day.
- **State Deadlines**: Many states align their deadlines with federal due dates, but specific requirements and deadlines can vary by state. It's important to check with your state tax agency for exact deadlines.
- **Extensions**: Filing for an extension typically provides more

time to submit tax forms but does not extend the time to pay taxes owed.

Consider setting reminders a few weeks in advance, or hiring a tax professional might be your best investment if you're unfamiliar with these forms.

3.4 APPLYING FOR BUSINESS CREDIT: A GUIDE FOR LLCS

Navigating the realm of business credit can sometimes feel like you're trying to crack an ancient code. But once you get the hang of it, you'll see it's more like having a superpower to amplify your business's potential and stability. Establishing and wisely using business credit not only boosts your LLC's financial health but also opens doors to better financing options and improves your business's image in the eyes of lenders and suppliers.

Think of business credit as your business's financial reputation—it tells lenders and vendors how responsible your business is with money. Just like a good personal credit score can help you secure loans and favorable interest rates, a solid business credit score can help your LLC get better loan terms, lower insurance premiums, and even negotiate better payment terms with suppliers. Essentially, it's about making your business look attractive on paper.

You build this credit over time. Begin by legally and adequately forming your business. Ensure you have everything in order, such as your business license, a dedicated business address, and the essential EIN. Next, open a business credit file with all three major business credit bureaus: Experian, Equifax, and Dun & Bradstreet. Like personal credit, each bureau can have slightly different information, so keeping an eye on all three is a good strategy.

Dun & Bradstreet (D&B): Known for its D-U-N-S Number and Paydex Score, D&B provides business credit information and ratings.

Experian Business: Offers business credit reports and scores, including the Experian Intelliscore Plus, which evaluates credit risk.

Equifax Business: Provides business credit reports and scores, including the Equifax Business Credit Risk Score, which assesses the likelihood of a business's payment performance.

Here's a crucial point: always pay your invoices on time. Although it might seem obvious, even one late payment can significantly dent your credit score in the business credit world. Consider setting up automated payments for your regular expenses to avoid any oversights. Moreover, strategically using a business credit card can help build your credit. Use it for regular expenses and pay it off monthly so your credit strengthens.

Securing loans and lines of credit is another scene where your newfound credit prowess can shine. When you're ready to take this step, preparation is critical. Lenders look at not just your credit score but also your business's financial health overall. They want to see profit and loss statements, cash flow details, and your business plan. Remember to present yourself in the best light and prove you've got what it takes to handle the money responsibly.

Before applying, ensure you understand the loan or credit line terms. What's the interest rate? Are there any fees? What's the repayment schedule? It's essential to avoid getting so caught up in securing the funds that you agree to terms that might hurt your business in the long run. Think of it as agreeing to the terms of a peace treaty—you want to ensure you're not setting yourself up for a stricter battle down the line.

Using credit responsibly is the final piece of the puzzle. Managing your debt levels ensures your business remains financially healthy. Only bite off what you can chew. High debt levels can strain your business's cash flow and damage your credit score if you still need payments. Also, keep an eye on interest rates—they can sneak up on you and suddenly turn a manageable debt into a financial nightmare.

Remember, the goal here isn't just to get access to credit; it's to use it to benefit your business strategically. Whether leveraging loans to expand your operations or using a business credit card to streamline your monthly expenses, credit is a powerful tool—if wielded correctly.

Visual Element: Checklist for Building Business Credit

1. **Legal Setup:** Ensure your business is legally registered and has all necessary licenses and permits.
2. **Open a Credit File**: Register with Experian, Equifax, and Dun & Bradstreet.
3. **Automate Payments**: Set up automated systems to ensure you never miss a bill payment.
4. **Use Business Credit Cards**: Make regular purchases and pay off the monthly balance.
5. **Monitor Your Credit:** Regularly check your credit reports for inaccuracies or potential fraud.
6. **Understand Loan Terms**: Before agreeing to any loan, fully understand the repayment terms and interest rates.

You are now equipped with the essentials of managing your LLC's finances—from opening the proper bank accounts to understanding the basics of business credit. With these tools in hand, you're better prepared to navigate the financial seas that lie ahead.

Remember, the goal of financial management isn't just to keep your business afloat but to ensure it thrives and grows. Next, we'll explore navigating state-specific LLC regulations, ensuring your business meets its financial goals and remains compliant with the ever-changing tapestry of laws and regulations.

4

NAVIGATING STATE-SPECIFIC LLC REGULATIONS

Choosing the right state to register your LLC can be challenging, as each state has its own set of rules and regulations. This chapter will guide you through the specifics of state-specific LLC regulations. We'll cover what you must verify to ensure your LLC remains compliant and avoids legal issues.

4.1 UNDERSTANDING AND NAVIGATING YOUR STATE'S LLC REGULATIONS

Researching State Requirements

Each state in the U.S. has a Secretary of State website. These websites are goldmines of information detailing everything you need to know about forming and running an LLC in that state. You'll want to start by typing "(Your State) Secretary of State" into your favorite search engine. Once you're on the site, look for the business or corporation's division. These websites can sometimes be challenging, so you should use the search bar to find specific information about LLCs. Most states have a section dedicated to business formations, which you should review.

Download all relevant PDFs on forming an LLC, and look for links to statutes or the state code if you want detailed information. Bookmark these pages, as you'll likely need to refer to them frequently.

Key Variations to Look For

As you're combing through this information, keep an eye out for a few things that vary wildly from state to state. Some states, like New York, require you to publish a notice in the newspaper about your new LLC. Other states might want you to file annual reports or pay franchise taxes, essentially the state's way of saying, "Thanks for doing business here; now pay up."

You'll also need to find out about any state-specific taxes. Beyond the usual income and sales taxes, some states have a personal property tax, a business license tax, or gross receipts tax based on your total revenue rather than your profit.

Staying Updated with Changes

Keeping up with legislative changes affecting LLCs in your state can be challenging, as new laws and regulations frequently arise. To stay informed, subscribe to newsletters from your state's Secretary of State or a trusted legal update service. These newsletters provide regular updates, allowing you to focus on running your business without constantly searching for legal information.

Utilizing Legal Expertise

No matter how savvy you are, sometimes you must call in the pros. Consulting with a local attorney specializing in business law can be a game-changer, especially when understanding and navigating the labyrinth of state-specific regulations. Think of it as having a local guide when you're hiking an unfamiliar trail. Sure, you could figure it out independently, but would you rather have someone who knows every twist and turn?

An attorney can provide personalized advice tailored to your situation and your state's legal landscape. They're convenient when drafting your Operating Agreement, ensuring it meets state requirements and aligns with your business goals and practices. Plus, they can help you comply with ongoing requirements, like annual reports and tax filings, which keeps your LLC in good standing and out of trouble.

Interactive Element: State-Specific Checklist

Navigating state-specific LLC regulations might not be the most thrilling part of running a business, but it's crucial. By conducting proper research, paying attention to details, and possibly seeking legal help, you can set yourself up to meet and master your state's requirements. So, take a deep breath, dive into those Secretary of State websites, and start piecing together your LLC's compliance puzzle—it's one of the first significant steps in setting your business up for long term success.

4.2 MULTI-STATE OPERATIONS: MANAGING LLC COMPLIANCE ACROSS BORDERS

After mastering the LLC regulations in your home state, consider expanding your business to other states. Expanding involves understanding and complying with the different state laws where you plan to operate. Let's explore what it takes to register and manage your LLC as a "foreign" entity in other states.

Registering as a Foreign LLC

When your LLC starts doing business in a state other than its home state, it is considered a "foreign" entity (no passport required). This term doesn't mean international; it's just how states refer to out-of-state businesses. To set up shop, you must register as a foreign LLC in each state where you're actively doing business. What counts as "doing business"? Well, it usually involves having a physical presence like a store, office, or warehouse or having significant sales in the state.

The process involves applying to the state's business entity registration office, usually the Secretary of State. You'll need to provide proof that your LLC is in good standing in its home state (like a Certificate of Good Standing) and details about your business. Are you skipping this step? Bad idea. It's like driving without a license; if caught, you could face fines, back taxes, and even get barred from doing business in the state altogether. So, keep it legal and keep it tidy.

Navigating Multiple Compliance Requirements

How do you manage compliance across various states? Start with a solid system to track the regulatory requirements in each state, including annual reports, tax filings, and any specific local compliance needs. Utilizing compliance software can be a game-changer here. These platforms act like your personal compliance concierge, reminding you of deadlines, helping you file the necessary paperwork, and keeping digital records of all your submissions. It's like having a personal assistant obsessed with details; in this game, details are everything.

Tax Considerations for Multi-State Operations

When you expand across state lines, tax complexity multiplies. Each state has its tax rules, and you'll likely need to deal with sales, income, and other state-specific taxes. The key term here is "**nexus**," which refers to your business's connection to a state, triggering tax obligations. You can establish nexus through physical presence, employees, or significant sales. To manage this, keep meticulous records of where you generate sales, hire employees, and maintain inventory.

This data is crucial for determining where you owe tax and how much. Consider working with a tax professional who specializes in multi-state operations. They can help navigate the turbulent waters of state tax regulations, ensuring you only pay what you need or fail to pay what you owe.

Practical Tips for Expansion

Do your homework before you plant your business flag in a new state. Each market is as unique as the locals' preference for their home team. Conduct thorough market research to understand regional consumer behaviors, economic conditions, and local competitors. It's not just about knowing if there's a demand for your products or services; it's about understanding how to communicate effectively with your new audience—what appeals to them and what doesn't.

Consider the logistical aspects of your expansion. If you're shipping goods, look into distribution channels and infrastructure. If you need a physical presence, think about real estate, employment laws, and local business networks that can support your growth. Always have a clear strategic plan outlining your goals, expected challenges, and how to meet them. This plan will guide your expansion and help convince potential investors or partners that you know what you're doing and are prepared to win big.

Expanding your LLC across state borders is a bold move—it's like playing chess on several boards at once. Each state's regulations add complexity to your operations. Still, you can navigate this multi-state maze with careful planning, the right tools, and a bit of entrepreneurial spirit. Remember, the goal isn't just to grow bigger but brighter, turning challenges into opportunities and new markets into home turf.

4.3 THE IMPACT OF LOCAL LAWS ON YOUR LLC OPERATIONS

Navigating local laws can be challenging, as each area has its own rules. However, understanding local zoning laws and licensing requirements is crucial for your LLC, ensuring your business operates legally and avoids issues.

Let's break down these local requirements so you can form your business correctly.

Local zoning laws are the gatekeepers of where and how businesses can operate. Think of them as the bouncers at the club. Depending on whether your business fits the neighborhood's "vibe," they can either wave you in or send you packing.

Zoning laws can dictate everything from the type of business you can run in certain areas to the signs you can put up and even where your customers can park. Before you sign a lease or buy property, you'll want to make a beeline to your local zoning office to get the lowdown on what's allowed. You will run into trouble if you dream of opening a swanky downtown nightclub in an area zoned for quiet retail shops. It's better to know before you invest!

Getting the necessary permits and licenses is another crucial step, akin to collecting all the right game pieces before you start playing. Depending on your business type and location, you might need anything from a basic business operation license to more specific permits, like health permits if you're opening a restaurant or a construction permit if you're planning to build. Your local city hall or county clerk's office is where you'll find the treasure map of information on what you need. And remember, the cost of these permits can vary as widely as lottery ticket prices, so factor these expenses into your budget.

Interacting effectively with local government officials can turn potential headaches into smooth sailing. Think of these folks as possible allies in your quest for business success. Building a good relationship can help you navigate the often-tedious bureaucratic processes more efficiently. Attend local business meetings, introduce yourself, and don't be shy about asking questions.

Regarding discussions or negotiations, whether permit fees or signage restrictions, keeping a friendly and open line of communication can make a difference. It's like knowing the secret handshake - it might not get you everything you want, but it'll open doors.

If you're feeling overwhelmed by all this, you're not alone. Thankfully, you don't have to navigate this complex landscape by yourself. Resources like local chambers of commerce, business advisory councils, and online forums can offer guidance and advice. These organizations are like having a navigator in the passenger seat; they can help you steer clear of potential pitfalls and connect you with other local business owners who've been in your shoes. They often have a wealth of information on the specific compliance requirements for your area. They can help you understand the finer points of local laws.

Understanding and complying with local laws seem daunting. Still, it's fundamental to setting up and successfully running your LLC. By taking the time to research, build relationships, and utilize available resources, you can ensure that your business meets local regulations and thrives because of your proactive efforts.

Remember, when it comes to local compliance, it's not just about following the rules—it's about weaving them into the fabric of your business practices to create a robust and resilient operation that stands the test of time. So, arm yourself with knowledge, reach out for help when needed, and prepare to make your business a beloved part of the local landscape.

4.4 CASE STUDY: SUCCESSFULLY SETTING UP AN LLC IN CALIFORNIA VS. NEW YORK

When setting up an LLC, think of California and New York as two very different beasts in the zoo of entrepreneurship. Both states offer vibrant markets and plenty of opportunities. Still, they come with rules, costs, and bureaucratic hoops. Let's look at how launching an LLC compares to these iconic locales.

Comparative Analysis

In California, the sun shines bright, and so does the potential for business growth. However, setting up an LLC here involves costs that can make your wallet feel lighter. The state requires an initial filing fee that's hefty compared to many other states, and there's also an annual franchise tax—a kind of "thanks for doing business here" fee.

On the flip side, New York asks for a filing fee that's on par with California but adds a quirky twist: the publication requirement. This old-school rule requires LLCs to announce their formation in two local newspapers, which can vary in cost depending on the county.

California processes LLC formations relatively quickly, often within a week if you file online. However, getting through all the red tape can still feel like trying to win a race on a skateboard. New York's processing times can be swift, especially with expedited options. Still, the publication requirement can drag the total setup time to over a month.

Navigational Challenges and Solutions

Each state has its peculiarities that can trip up the unprepared entrepreneur. In California, one common challenge is navigating the complex web of regulations that can vary widely by locality, not just by state. For instance, if you're in the tech industry, you'll need to be keenly aware of privacy laws that can impact how you operate.

Meanwhile, New York throws its curveballs in the form of stringent labor laws and safety regulations, which can be a minefield for new business owners who need to become more familiar with the specifics.

The key to success in each state is proactive planning and local know-how. Many successful LLCs in California make it a point to invest in legal and consultancy services upfront to ensure they fully comply with state and local regulations. In New York, savvy entrepreneurs often leverage local business development centers and legal clinics to get up-to-speed on the unique requirements of the state and city.

Impact of State-Specific Features on Business

Both states are known for their high tax rates, which can eat into profits. However, they balance this with many resources and incentives for small businesses, including grants, loans, and programs designed to foster innovation and entrepreneurship. These features can significantly impact the success and operations of an LLC, offering substantial support but also requiring businesses to stay on top of their tax planning and financial management.

Moreover, these states offer robust consumer markets and access to a diverse talent pool. An advantage for any LLC is that you can navigate the regulatory and tax landscapes effectively. The key is thoroughly understanding how these state-specific features can impact your business model and plan accordingly.

Lessons Learned

The tales of LLCs carving out successful niches in California and New York teach us a few universal lessons. First, understanding and adapting to local regulations is crucial. What works in one state may not work in another, and assuming otherwise can be costly. Second, leverage state-specific benefits. Both states offer unique advantages that, when used wisely, can significantly aid in business growth.

Finally, always plan for the long term. California and New York can be challenging environments in which to do business. Still, they also offer tremendous opportunities for those navigating their complexities. Strategic planning, a solid understanding of local laws and taxes, and a proactive approach to compliance are essential to turning these challenges into stepping stones for success.

This exploration of creating LLCs in California versus New York highlights the importance of state-specific considerations. It underscores the broader theme of adaptability and informed decision-making in business. As we turn the page to the next chapter, we'll delve deeper into maintaining compliance and leveraging state-specific advantages, ensuring your LLC survives and thrives in the dynamic landscape of American business.

5

PROTECTING YOUR ASSETS

Protecting your assets under an LLC is crucial for maintaining your business's financial health. Think of your LLC as a secure building where your business operations run smoothly and your assets are safely stored. Your asset protection strategy acts as the walls of this building, designed to keep threats like creditors and lawsuits away. However, more than just one layer of protection is optional. You need multiple layers to ensure your assets remain secure.

Let's explore how to fortify your LLC effectively.

5.1 ASSET PROTECTION STRATEGIES FOR LLC OWNERS

Utilizing the LLC Structure for Protection

The LLC, or Limited Liability Company, isn't just a fancy business designation—it's a shield for your assets. This structure legally separates your goodies (like your home, car, and comic book collection you've hoarded since childhood) from your business liabilities. Consider it as having an invisible force field that keeps your assets safe if your business faces legal action.

Let's say your LLC is in a lawsuit because a customer slipped on a banana peel in your office (who left that there, anyway?). The lawsuit can go after your business assets—your office, business bank accounts, etc.—but thanks to the legal magic of the LLC, your assets are off-limits.

Enhancing Protection through Multiple LLCs

What if you're an entrepreneur who loves juggling multiple projects? You might have a café on one side of town, a boutique on the other, and a new tech startup brewing in your garage.

Here's a pro tip: use multiple LLCs to compartmentalize risks. If the café faces a lawsuit, the liabilities don't spill over to affect your boutique or tech venture. Each business is its legal entity with its separate liability shield.

This strategy is particularly savvy for real estate investors who own multiple properties—putting each property in a separate LLC keeps the risks isolated, minimizing the domino effect if things go south with one investment.

Importance of Formality and Compliance

The effectiveness of an LLC in protecting your assets depends on treating it as a separate entity by keeping meticulous records, holding regular meetings (even if it's just you), and following all the formalities required by state law. Maintaining these practices is essential to ensure your LLC's protections remain strong.

Moreover, staying compliant involves more than just paperwork. It's about understanding and adhering to the laws that govern LLCs in your state. Each state has its quirks; slipping up on a technicality can weaken your liability shield, making your assets vulnerable.

Avoiding Piercing the Corporate Veil

One significant risk to your asset protection strategy is "*piercing the corporate veil.*" This sounds dramatic because courts can decide that your LLC doesn't exist separate from you personally, usually because you must follow the necessary formalities or have mixed personal and business finances (commingling). When this happens, bye-bye force field—creditors can go after your assets.

To avoid this:

1. Keep your business and personal finances distinctly separate.
2. Open separate bank accounts, and never use your business account to pay for personal expenses (no, that new T.V. for the living room is not a business expense).
3. Ensure you fund your business. Treating the LLC like a personal piggy bank is asking for trouble.

Visual Element: LLC Compliance Checklist

To keep your LLC's liability shield strong and your asset protection strategies effective, here's a handy checklist to keep you on track:

1. **Separate Finances**: Maintain clear boundaries between personal and business finances.
2. **Hold Annual Meetings:** Document decisions and policies discussed and agreed upon, even if you're a solo act.
3. **Follow State Laws**: Keep abreast of changes in your state's LLC laws to ensure compliance.
4. **Document Everything:** From major decisions to daily transactions, keep records that reflect your business operations separate from your dealings.

By following these strategies, you are protecting your assets and ensuring that your LLC serves its primary purpose: to be a safe, structured, and legally compliant entity for your business ventures.

With your protections in place and your assets secure, you can focus on growing your business.

5.2 THE ROLE OF INSURANCE IN PROTECTING YOUR LLC

Navigating the treacherous waters of business risks without insurance is like a tightrope walking without a net—thrilling, yes, but unwise. Let's unpack the different types of insurance you might consider to keep your LLC not just standing but thriving, even when the unexpected hits.

Types of Insurance for LLCs

General liability insurance is like your business's everyday armor. It protects against claims of bodily injury or property damage caused by your business activities. Imagine a customer visiting your office trips over a rug and decides to sue. General liability can cover medical bills and legal fees, which can be a financial lifesaver. Then there's professional liability insurance, also known as errors and omissions (E&O) insurance. This one's crucial if your business provides services or advice.

Let's say you're a consultant, and your advice turned out to be less than stellar, costing your client a hefty sum. Professional liability can cover the legal costs and damages, keeping your financial boat afloat.

Property insurance should also be on your radar, especially if your business owns physical assets like computers, furniture, or specialized equipment. It covers damage to your business property from fire, theft, and, sometimes, natural disasters. Think of it as a fortress protecting your physical assets from the marauders of the real world.

If your business involves manufacturing or you own a storefront, this type of insurance isn't just helpful; it's essential.

Assessing Insurance Needs

Assessing your insurance needs is about something other than guessing what could go wrong; it's about preparing for any potential possibilities. Start by evaluating the risks inherent in your industry. Are you in construction? Liability and property insurance are must-haves. Are you running an IT firm? Cyber liability should be at the top of your list, protecting you against data breaches or cyber-attacks.

Consider the scale of your operations, too. A home-based business might need less coverage than a business with a physical location or multiple employees. Consulting with an insurance broker can demystify this process. These professionals can provide a tailored risk assessment and guide you through myriad options, ensuring you get coverage that matches your business's risk profile without paying for unnecessary extras. Think of them as personal shoppers, but they are a perfect blend of expertise and tailored advice for your business security needs.

Integrating Insurance with LLC Protection

While your LLC structure offers a legal shield protecting personal assets from business liabilities, insurance adds an extra layer of security. In industries where litigation is common, such as healthcare or real estate, having robust insurance policies can be as crucial as the business model itself.

Insurance doesn't just cover potential liabilities; it also provides peace of mind, allowing you to focus on growing your business rather than fretting over potential threats. Moreover, certain contracts or business deals often require specific types of insurance. Not only does this assure your clients or partners of your professionalism, but it also enhances your business's credibility. It shows that you take risk management seriously and are prepared for unforeseen circumstances, making your business a reliable player in any industry.

Case Studies of Insurance Claims

To bring this all home, let's look at some real-life scenarios. Consider a tech startup that neglected to invest in cyber liability insurance. A data breach exposed customer data, leading to hefty fines and lawsuits. The financial burden was overwhelming; without insurance, they exposed their operations to significant risks.

Conversely, a small artisan bakery invested in a comprehensive property insurance policy. When a kitchen fire caused significant damage, the insurance covered the repairs and equipment replacement. The bakery was back in business quickly, with minimal financial disruption.

These examples underscore the importance of having insurance and the right kind of insurance. Whether it's a slip-and-fall lawsuit, a professional error, or a natural disaster, having the right insurance policies in place can mean the difference between a minor setback and a major catastrophe. So, consider your options, assess your risks, and don't hesitate to bring in the experts.

With the right insurance, your LLC can confidently navigate the choppiest of waters, knowing that your business is protected no matter the storm.

5.3 SEPARATING PERSONAL AND BUSINESS FINANCES: HOW AND WHY

Let's be honest. Mixing personal and business finances might seem convenient, but it can quickly become problematic. Clear boundaries between them are essential for your LLC. Start with the basics: opening a business bank account is fundamental in legitimizing and protecting your business.

Setting up a business bank account is surprisingly straightforward, akin to a personal account, but with a few more hoops. First, you'll need your business documentation in hand—think of these as your entry tickets, which include your EIN (Employer Identification Number), which acts like your business's social security number, and your Articles of Organization, which is like your LLC's birth certificate. With these documents, you're ready to approach a bank. Choose one that offers benefits tailored to business needs, such as low transaction fees or high transaction limits, depending on what your business operations might demand.

Next, consider the importance of this separation. By distinguishing between personal and business finances, you create a buffer that protects your assets from business liabilities. If your company ever faces legal issues, this separation makes it straightforward to creditors and courts that your finances should remain untouched. It simplifies your financial management, too. Imagine trying to sift through a mixed heap of personal and business transactions at tax time—keeping them separate makes your financial landscape more accessible to navigate and manage.

Now, onto using business credit cards. These are not just for racking up points or saving on business travel. There are powerful tools for organizing and separating your business expenditures from personal spending. Use them for everything from office supplies to client dinners. This approach simplifies tracking and reconciling expenses and strengthens your business credit history, benefiting future credit applications or business deals. It's like keeping a detailed diary of your business adventures, financially speaking.

You must address the legal implications of maintaining this separation. In the eyes of the law, and particularly for tax purposes, your LLC is considered a separate entity. Commingling funds or treating your business bank account like your personal piggy bank can lead to what's known as 'piercing the corporate veil.' The legal term "piercing the corporate veil" is as dramatic as it sounds—it means that a court could compromise the legal protection provided by the LLC structure, thereby exposing the owner's assets to potential lawsuits or creditors.

For practical financial management, start by leveraging technology. Accounting software can be your best friend, automating the tracking of income and expenses while integrating directly with your bank accounts and credit cards. Using such software minimizes errors and provides real-time insights into your financial health. Regular reviews of these financial statements can help you catch issues early, adjust strategies promptly, and make informed business decisions.

Another tip is hiring a professional accountant, especially if finance isn't someone else's forte. Consider an accountant your financial navigator, helping steer your business through complex tax laws and financial planning strategies. They can ensure that your financial practices comply with legal requirements and support your business goals and growth.

Keeping your personal and business finances distinct sets a strong foundation for your LLC's financial health and stability. It's about creating a system that supports your business's growth and safeguards your financial well-being. So, take the time to set up those accounts, use the right financial tools, and keep a keen eye on the separation. Your future self will thank you.

5.4 INVESTING IN YOUR FUTURE: PERSONAL FINANCE FOR LLC OWNERS

So, you've launched your LLC, and it's rolling along like a well-oiled machine. But have you thought about what happens when it's time to hang up your entrepreneurial hat? Or even before then, when you want to take that dream vacation without fretting about business expenses? That's where intelligent personal investing comes into play. Think of it as planting a garden where your future self can harvest the rewards, whether sipping margaritas on a beach or enjoying a comfy retirement.

Investing in the future is crucial, not just for your personal life but also for a savvy business move. It ensures you're not wholly dependent on the success of your LLC. Diversifying your financial portfolio is like having different streams that fill your lake. Even if one stream dries up, you've got others to keep the water levels stable. Let's dive into the world of retirement accounts and other investment options that can help secure your financial future beyond the day-to-day grind of business management.

Exploring Retirement Accounts

There are several types of retirement accounts to consider, each with its own rules and benefits. A *Roth IRA*, for instance, is like planting a seed that grows tax-free; you pay taxes when you put money in, but not when you take it out during retirement. Paying taxes upfront is especially beneficial if you expect to be in a higher tax bracket later on because you will pay lower taxes now than you would on the growth in the future. Then there's the *Traditional IRA*, which is more like a deferred payment plan. You get a tax deduction when you contribute, which can be helpful if you need to reduce your taxable income now.

A *SEP IRA* (Simplified Employee Pension) or a Solo 401(k) might increase your speed for self-employed or running small businesses. These accounts allow you to contribute significantly more than traditional IRAs, aligning nicely with higher income years. Think of a Solo 401(k) as your personal savings powerhouse, letting you play employee and employer, maximizing your retirement contributions and tax benefits.

Setting up these accounts requires careful planning. You should consider factors like contribution limits, tax implications, and your current and future financial situation. Each decision impacts how much you can save and how your funds will grow. Think of it as creating a plan tailored to your financial goals.

Diversifying Investment Options

While retirement accounts are fantastic, they're just one piece of the puzzle. Diversifying your investments is about not putting all your eggs in one basket—or, in this case, not all your money in one type of asset. Stocks, bonds, mutual funds, real estate, and more can all contribute to a well-rounded investment strategy.

Stocks can be exciting with the potential for high returns, but they can also be risky. Bonds are usually safer and more reliable but offer lower returns. Mutual funds provide a balanced mix of stocks, bonds, and other assets managed by experts. Real estate is a tangible way to build wealth through rental income or property appreciation. Each investment type has risks and rewards, so consider what combination suits you. It's all about finding a balance that aligns with your financial goals and comfort level.

Setting Up Automated Contributions

One of the smartest moves you can make is setting up automated contributions to your investment accounts. It's like setting a fitness goal, where consistency is vital. Automating your savings ensures regular contributions and applies a principle called dollar-cost averaging, which can reduce the impact of market volatility. Plus, it's less painful than watching large chunks of money leave your account manually. You can set it, forget it, and watch your investments grow.

Tax Benefits of Personal Investments

The tax benefits of investing can be sweet. Many retirement accounts offer tax advantages, whether tax-deferral or tax-free growth. Understanding these can help you plan for retirement and tax efficiency each year. Contributions to traditional IRAs lower your taxable income now, while Roth options could provide tax-free income later. It's like choosing between paying for express shipping or getting a rebate on a delayed delivery—both have perks, depending on your immediate needs and plans.

Consulting Financial Advisors

Lastly, take into account the value of professional advice. A good financial advisor can be like a navigator for your investment journey, helping you avoid pitfalls and discover opportunities you might not have considered. They can tailor an investment strategy that fits your personal and business financial goals, risk tolerance, and life plans. Whether planning for early retirement, saving for your kids' education, or just building a safety net, a financial advisor can provide the expertise and guidance to help you make informed decisions.

Investing in your future is not just about stashing away money; it's about making strategic choices that ensure you can enjoy life, both now and later, without financial stress. Whether through savvy retirement planning, a diversified investment portfolio, or intelligent tax strategies, taking control of your finances is crucial to managing your LLC. It's about securing not just your business's future but your own. So, take the time to explore your options, set up intelligent systems, and consider seeking expert advice.

Your future self will appreciate the effort, enjoying a worry-free life and the fruits of your careful planning.

5.5 LEGAL SAFEGUARDS TO ENHANCE YOUR LLC'S ASSET PROTECTION

When running your LLC, legal safeguards are crucial for keeping your operations smooth and secure. One of the first steps is crafting solid contracts. A well-drafted contract is not just a formal agreement; it's your first line of defense if disputes arise. It sets clear boundaries and expectations for all parties involved. Ensure each contract includes vital elements such as the rights and responsibilities of all parties, payment terms, confidentiality clauses, and conditions for termination. These components should be as specific as possible to avoid ambiguity, often leading to disputes. Always have a lawyer review your contracts before you sign them to ensure they are solid and practical.

Regular legal audits are another critical defense strategy. Think of these as your business's regular health check-ups; they help diagnose issues before they become serious. At least once a year, review your business practices and ensure they comply with current laws and regulations. Ensure that your company follows proper hiring practices, follows safety regulations, and correctly files taxes. Regular audits can help you identify potential legal vulnerabilities early, allowing you to fix them before they become costly legal battles.

Non-Disclosure Agreements (NDAs) are your secret keepers. They protect sensitive business information, such as trade secrets, business plans, and client data, from being leaked to competitors or the public. Whether discussing a potential business deal or hiring a new employee with access to critical data, having an NDA is like having a lock on your private diary. It ensures that the parties involved understand the importance of confidentiality and are legally bound to respect it.

Lastly, remember to protect your digital assets. In today's tech-driven world, data breaches can be financially disastrous for your business's reputation. Implement robust data security measures to safeguard your business information, including using strong passwords, encrypting sensitive data, and securing your networks. Additionally, if your business is subject to regulations like the General Data Protection Regulation (GDPR) or the Health Insurance Portability and Accountability Act (HIPAA), comply with these laws to avoid hefty fines. Data security is not just about protecting information; it's about protecting your business's integrity and trustworthiness.

Integrating these legal safeguards into your LLC's operations protects your business from threats. It builds a foundation of trust with your clients and partners. It's about being proactive rather than reactive, ensuring your business thrives in a secure and compliant environment. With your legal defenses set, you can focus on what you do best —running your business and pushing toward its growth and success.

As we move into the next phase of our journey, we will explore navigating the complexities of compliance and legal issues to ensure that your LLC survives and thrives in the dynamic landscape of modern business.

The Complete LLC Guide For Beginners

Daily Management/ Growth Strategies
***

T.J. Griffin

6

DAILY OPERATIONS AND MANAGEMENT

The daily grind of running your LLC involves effectively managing your projects, team, and finances. To succeed, you need solid management practices, valuable tools, and effective delegation. Let's dive into turning your everyday tasks into a well-coordinated and successful operation.

6.1 EFFECTIVE DAILY MANAGEMENT PRACTICES FOR YOUR LLC

Establishing Routine Processes

Think of your business as a well-run operation where established systems and procedures are essential. While flexibility can foster creativity, too much chaos can disrupt operations. Establishing routine processes ensures that your business runs smoothly, even when you're not there to oversee every detail.

Start with the basics: bookkeeping, customer communications, and inventory management. These foundational tasks are essential for keeping your business organized and efficient. Use software like

QuickBooks or Sage Business Cloud Accounting for bookkeeping to capture every transaction quickly and efficiently.

For customer communications, set up templates and standards for everything from emails to social media posts, ensuring your business voice stays consistent and clear. And for inventory? Get a system that tracks your stock faster than you can say "out of stock." The goal is to create a clear playbook so anyone on your team can manage day-to-day operations efficiently and without confusion.

Utilizing Management Tools

If you have a secret twin, you can only be in multiple places at once, and that's where management tools and software come in—they effectively clone your managerial skills. There's a tool for almost every aspect of business management, from project management dashboards that keep your projects on track (and show who's dropping the ball) to CRM systems that manage customer relationships as smoothly as a top-tier concierge.

Consider tools like Asana or Trello for project tracking; they're like having a digital production manager who never sleeps. For customer relationship management, systems like Salesforce can make personalizing customer interactions a breeze. Let's remember financial tools like QuickBooks or Sage, which can help keep your finances organized and accurate. The right tools save you time and ensure your operations run smoothly.

Delegation and Team Management

Delegation is a skill. When done correctly, it empowers your team and allows you to focus on growth. When done well, it can lead to clarity and communication. The key is to know which tasks to delegate and to whom. Some team members have different skills, and that's perfectly fine. Assign tasks based on their strengths and areas for development to ensure that each team member is well-suited for the given tasks.

Once you've delegated, communication is your best friend. Be clear about expectations, deadlines, and the scope of work. Regular check-ins help keep everyone on track, and providing routine feedback is essential. Delegation isn't just about assigning tasks; it's about offering guidance and fostering growth.

Monitoring Performance

Finally, monitoring the performance of your business and team is crucial. Establish systems to track both, such as performance metrics for business operations and regular reviews for your team. This approach ensures that your business is meeting customer expectations and operating efficiently.

Use tools to get real-time data on business performance. Analytics can show which products fly off the shelves or which services garner reviews. Employee performance tools can reveal who is excelling and who may need additional coaching to reach their full potential.

Visual Element: Interactive Management Dashboard Example

Here's an interactive dashboard example to give you a taste of effective management. Imagine a screen showing real-time metrics on sales, customer engagement, and inventory levels alongside staff performance reviews and project progress. It's like having a command center at your fingertips.

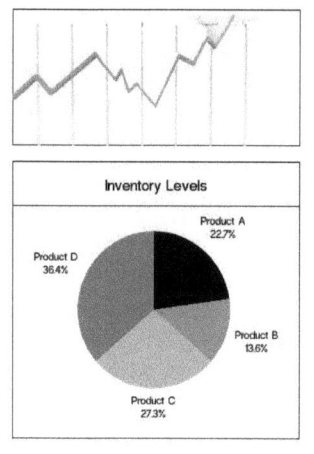

Managing your LLC's day-to-day operations can be smooth. You can run your business efficiently and effectively with solid processes, the right tools, and effective delegation.

Good performance monitoring will help keep your business on track and identify opportunities for success. Aim for excellence to keep driving your business forward.

6.2 HIRING EMPLOYEES VS. CONTRACTORS: WHAT LLCS NEED TO KNOW

When managing an LLC, deciding between hiring employees and engaging contractors is crucial. Both options can meet your needs, but each has legal and tax implications. Understanding these differences can save you from potential issues and ensure you make the right choice for your business.

Let's break down the legal and tax details. When you hire an employee, you have more control over their work and performance, which comes with additional responsibilities, such as withholding income taxes, paying Social Security and Medicare taxes, and contributing to unemployment and workers' compensation insurance. Although this involves more paperwork and higher operational costs, it also ensures loyalty and consistency in your workforce.

On the flip side, contractors are more like hiring a guest soloist. They bring their style, use their tools, and operate independently from your business. They handle their taxes (you whip out a 1099 form at the end of the year), and generally, you pay them either per project or at an hourly rate agreed upon. The catch? You need more control over how they work, which can be a no-go if you want to build a consistent brand experience.

Now, diving deeper into the pros and cons, hiring employees means investing in training and development, which can boost your team's overall productivity and business growth. However, it's a long-term commitment. Think pension plans, health insurance, and other benefits. Contractors, though, are more like hiring a landscaping service. They come in, get the job done, and leave. It's simpler, but remember, they can be less invested in your business's long-term success.

When it comes to compliance, things become more complex if you have employees. Ensuring fair labor practices, adhering to employment laws, and correctly handling payroll taxes requires careful attention to detail. Missing any steps can lead to significant issues. On the other hand, managing contractors is generally more straightforward. Ensure the contract clearly outlines the scope of work, deadlines, and payment terms. However, it's crucial to ensure they are genuinely contractors and not employees misclassified as contractors, as this can lead to legal problems.

Whether you're hiring employees or contractors, clarity is your best friend. Start with clear job descriptions that outline expectations and responsibilities. When interviewing, ask questions that fit the position and ensure that the candidate aligns with your company culture. And when you've found your match, onboard them properly. For employees, this means a thorough introduction to your company, their role, and their benefits. It means ensuring contractors clearly understand the project, deadlines, and contact points.

Navigating the hiring process sets the tone for your working relationships. Whether you're establishing a long-term connection with an employee or a temporary, project-based arrangement with a contractor, each role plays a crucial part in the growth and flexibility of your LLC. Choose wisely and prepare thoroughly, as your team will be an instrumental part of your business every step of the way.

6.3 IMPLEMENTING STANDARD OPERATING PROCEDURES (SOPS) IN YOUR LLC

Think of Standard Operating Procedures (SOPs) as your business's playbook. These documents are essential for ensuring consistency and quality in your operations. SOPs ensure that everyone on your team performs tasks similarly, always maintaining the same standards. They are crucial for smooth and efficient business operations, ensuring that your business runs seamlessly regardless of who is working.

Why should you bother with SOPs? First off, they cut through the chaos. Imagine training every new employee with a different set of instructions—sounds like a recipe for a migraine, right? SOPs lay down the law; they're your business commandments. Everyone follows the same procedures, which means consistency in your business's operations, no matter who's at the helm. This consistency is critical to quality control, ensuring your products or services remain top-notch, which keeps customers returning for more. Plus, well-documented SOPs can be huge time-savers. They reduce the training time for new staff because everything they need to know is clear with easy-to-follow steps.

Developing effective SOPs starts with identifying the tasks that need standardization. Look at your daily operations and pinpoint areas where inconsistencies appear. It could involve handling customer complaints, checking inventory, or documenting the end-of-day cash flow. Once you've identified these tasks, then it's time to report them. Start as if you're explaining the process to someone who has never stepped foot in your industry. Keep your instructions clear and straightforward. Use bullet points or numbered steps to make the procedures easy to follow, and where necessary, add diagrams or screenshots—it's like adding illustrations to a how-to book, making it easier to grasp.

While you're the maestro orchestrating this, involve your team in the SOP development process. They're in the trenches and might have insights or shortcuts you still need to consider. Involving them in the process improves the SOPs and fosters team buy-in, as they are more likely to follow procedures they helped create.

Training Employees on SOPs

Once your SOPs are ready, they're only as good as the accompanying training. You can't just toss a 50-page manual at your employees and say, "Go read this." It would help if you walked them through it, showed them the process, and then let them try their hands with you guiding them. Use a mix of training methods—demonstrations, one-on-one sessions, group discussions, and even quizzes—to ensure the information sticks.

Training shouldn't be a one-and-done deal. Make it an ongoing part of your business culture. Regularly schedule refresher sessions to ensure old and new staff stay within the established procedures. Always make yourself or a seasoned employee available to answer any questions. This open-door policy helps maintain your set standards and ensures that SOPs are more than just formalities; they are integral to your operations.

Review and Update SOPs

Here's something crucial—SOPs are not set in stone. As your business evolves, so should your SOPs. Make it a habit to review them at least once a year. Are there new tools or technologies that could make the processes more efficient? Have there been changes in compliance or regulatory requirements? Or maybe you've just discovered a better way of doing things. Whatever the case, updating your SOPs ensures they keep pace with your business's growth and the ever-changing market landscape.

To address this critical responsibility adequately, set up a review committee or assign the task to a trusted manager. They can gather feedback from the team, assess the effectiveness of each SOP, and make recommendations for changes. Remember, the goal of this review isn't just to tweak documents—it's to continually enhance and streamline how your business operates, ensuring you remain agile and competitive.

Implementing and maintaining SOPs might seem daunting, but it can significantly streamline your operations, maintain quality control, and boost efficiency. It's about investing in your business's operational excellence—an investment that pays dividends by saving time, maintaining standards, and simplifying training. Creating SOPs will transform your daily operations into a harmonious and efficient system, ensuring consistency and excellence.

6.4 CRISIS MANAGEMENT: KEEPING YOUR LLC STABLE IN TOUGH TIMES

Imagine you're sailing smoothly on your entrepreneurial journey, and suddenly, a storm hits—your website crashes during a major sale, a natural disaster disrupts your supply chain, or a P.R. issue goes viral. Whether dramatic or minor, Crises can threaten your business if you're unprepared; let's discuss equipping your LLC with the necessary tools and strategies to stay stable during challenging times.

Identifying Potential Crises

The first step in crisis management is recognizing what could go wrong. Start by conducting a thorough risk assessment. Look at every aspect of your business, from I.T. systems and financial health to supply chains and employee dynamics. Identifying potential financial troubles that could stem from cash flow problems, technological failures like a hacked customer database, or external threats like new regulations or natural disasters can help you prepare effectively. It's like checking the weather before heading to sea; you might not change the ocean's mood, but you can decide whether to sail.

Developing a Crisis Management Plan

With potential threats identified, the next step is to craft a robust crisis management plan. This plan should outline specific steps in response to various scenarios and detail who on your team is responsible for each task. Assign roles and responsibilities, establish communication strategies for your team, and reach out to customers and stakeholders. Precise and reliable communication is essential for navigating the challenges in a crisis.

Set up contingency plans for different types of emergencies. For technology failures, have backup systems in place. For supply chain disruptions, identify alternative suppliers. Financial instability? Line up emergency funding sources. Each plan should include detailed response strategies, recovery steps, and a method for testing these plans regularly. It's not enough to have a lifeboat; you need to ensure it doesn't leak.

Effective Communication During Crises

When a crisis strikes, how you communicate can make or break your business's ability to weather the storm. Internally, keep your team informed with regular updates. A well-informed crew is more effective and can function autonomously if communication lines get disrupted. Externally, manage your narrative carefully. Address public relations issues swiftly and transparently—this helps maintain trust and can prevent the crisis from spiraling out of control.

Whether it's a press release, a social media post, or a direct email to clients, ensure your messages are clear and address the issue head-on.

Learning from Crises

Finally, no matter how daunting, every crisis is an opportunity to learn and fortify your business against future storms. After navigating through a crisis, thoroughly review how your team and plans performed. What worked well? What faltered? Gather feedback from all levels of your organization and analyze the data to find valuable insights. Use this information to tighten your strategies, patch any overlooked vulnerabilities, and strengthen your crisis management framework.

Crises are inevitable, but collapse is not. By identifying potential threats, preparing a detailed crisis management plan, communicating effectively during emergencies, and learning from each incident, your LLC can survive and emerge more robust, more resilient, and ready to sail into smoother waters.

As we close this chapter on managing your LLC day-to-day and through crises, remember that your business's stability in tough times hinges on preparation, agility, and the ability to learn from past challenges. These strategies are life rafts, ensuring your business can navigate safely and effectively when storms hit. Up next, we'll explore growth strategies for your LLC, turning calm seas into opportunities for expansion and success.

YOUR JOURNEY TO BUSINESS SUCCESS WITH AN LLC

MAKE A DIFFERENCE WITH YOUR REVIEW

"Success is not final; failure is not fatal: It is the courage to continue that counts."

— WINSTON CHURCHILL

Understanding the intricacies of LLCs can feel overwhelming. *"The Complete LLC Guide for Beginners"* demystifies this process, empowering you to confidently set up and manage your LLC.

So far, we've covered the basics of LLC formation, from understanding what an LLC is to filing your Articles of Organization and drafting an Operating Agreement. These chapters lay a solid foundation for your business.

As you reach this midpoint, reflect on how these insights transform your business approach. The clarity and confidence gained here are invaluable tools for any entrepreneur. Whether starting or restructuring, this guide is designed to help you avoid pitfalls and succeed.

Please help that aspiring business owner by leaving this book a review.

Your gift costs no money and takes less than 60 seconds to make real, but it can change a fellow entrepreneur's life forever.

Your feedback is crucial for improving this guide. By leaving a review on Amazon, you help future entrepreneurs discover this resource and contribute to the success of small businesses. Share how this book has helped you and what others can expect to find.

Simply scan the QR code below to leave your review:
https://www.amazon.com/review/create-review?&asin=B0DMTQFGPM

I'm much more excited to help you achieve your business goals faster and easier than you imagine. You'll love the strategies I'm about to share in the coming chapters.

- *Fun fact:* If you provide something of value to another person, it makes you more valuable to them. If you'd like goodwill straight from another entrepreneur - and believe this book will help them - send it their way.

Thank you so much in advance.

I'm really looking forward to your valuable feedback!

Your biggest fan,   *T. J. Griffin*

Now, back to our regularly scheduled programming...

7

GROWTH STRATEGIES FOR LLCS

Growth is an exciting prospect for any entrepreneur. It's about increasing revenue and implementing intelligent, sustainable strategies that advance your business while managing your resources. Achieving growth involves carefully planned steps that ensure your business can expand and thrive steadily, balancing ambition and practicality.

7.1 ORGANIC GROWTH STRATEGIES FOR SMALL LLCS

Customer Retention Techniques

Attracting new customers and retaining them are essential aspects of your business. It's about providing ongoing value that keeps them coming back. Start by improving your customer service, such as ensuring your customer service team is responsive and helpful or using chatbots on your website for instant assistance. A satisfied customer is likelier to return and recommend your brand to others.

Implementing loyalty programs can also work wonders. Whether it's a punch card system where the tenth coffee is free or a points program that rewards customers for every dollar spent, find what resonates with your clientele. It's like feeding a treat to your pet; it keeps them delighted and coming back for more.

Remember the power of feedback. Regularly gather customer opinions through surveys or feedback forms. Utilize the collected insights to refine your offerings and address any concerns. Doing so improves customer satisfaction and makes them feel valued and heard, reinforcing their loyalty to your brand.

Increasing Operational Efficiency

Increasing operational efficiency is fine-tuning your processes to maximize productivity and reduce waste. Start with your supply chain—ensure it's as streamlined as possible. Negotiate with suppliers, keep inventory at optimal levels, and always have a backup plan in case of supply disruptions.

Automating routine tasks can also save you time and reduce errors. Whether it's automating invoice generation, customer follow-ups, or even social media posts, every little bit of automation helps you focus more on strategic tasks. It's like setting up automatic sprinklers for your garden; it keeps things flourishing without constant oversight.

Let's not forget the gold mine, which is data analytics. You can make informed decisions that push your business forward by tracking and analyzing your business data—from sales figures and website traffic to customer engagement metrics. It's like having a map and compass in the wilderness; it shows you where you are and helps guide you to where you want to be.

Product or Service Expansion

Expanding your range of products or services attracts new customers and generates interest in your business. However, before making any additions, assessing market demand is essential. Conduct market research, gather customer feedback, and test new ideas on a small scale to ensure they meet the needs of your audience.

Quality control is crucial when introducing new products or services. Ensure they meet the high standards your customers expect, which may require investing in better materials, advanced technology, or additional staff training. Maintaining quality will help you successfully expand and satisfy your customers' expectations.

Geographical Expansion

Expanding geographically can open up new markets and bring fresh opportunities. But before you pack your bags and set up shop in a new location, do your homework. Understand the latest market's culture, consumer behavior, and economic conditions. It's like learning the local language and customs before moving to a new country; it helps you blend in and connect better.

Consider the logistical aspects of expansion, too. How will you manage distribution, marketing, and customer service in a new area? What local regulations and licensing requirements will you need to comply with? It's akin to planning a road trip; you need a good map, a reliable vehicle, and an understanding of the traffic laws.

Expanding your LLC doesn't have to be a leap into the unknown. You can achieve significant growth without overextending yourself by implementing effective strategies for customer retention, operational efficiency, product expansion, and geographical growth. Stay informed, focus on your goals, and maintain smooth business operations. With these approaches, there's no limit to how far your LLC can go.

Ready to accelerate your business growth? Let's bring that vision to life.

7.2 EXPLORING MERGERS AND ACQUISITIONS: IS IT RIGHT FOR YOUR LLC?

When thinking about mergers and acquisitions (M&A), you might imagine large corporations making multimillion-dollar deals. However, M&A can also apply to your LLC in a more relatable way. Think of it as a strategic collaboration—either partnering with another business to enhance your offerings or bringing in new expertise to innovate and grow. Both approaches can significantly improve your business but require careful planning and execution for success.

Mergers and acquisitions, though often grouped, are distinct business strategies. A merger occurs when two companies, such as your LLC and another, combine into a single entity, pooling resources, clients, and strengths. An acquisition involves your LLC taking over another business and integrating it into your existing operations. The process can range from straightforwardly buying out a smaller competitor to strategically acquiring a company with complementary technology or market presence.

Finding the right business to merge with or acquire requires careful consideration. Evaluate potential targets' financial health, market position, and cultural fit. For example, if your LLC has a laid-back, innovative work environment, taking over a rigid, traditional company could create cultural clashes.

The M&A process involves several critical steps:

1. **Due Diligence**: Thoroughly investigate the target company's operations, financials, legal issues, etc. This phase helps ensure no unpleasant surprises after the deal is closed.
2. **Negotiating Terms**: Beyond the purchase price, negotiate the terms of integration, responsibilities, and future roles. Legal and financial advisors are essential to protect your business interests during this stage.

3. **Post-Acquisition Integration**: Successfully merging two businesses or integrating a new acquisition requires clear communication, meticulous planning, and patience. Align business processes, merge corporate cultures, and ensure smooth transitions.

Legal and financial considerations are crucial throughout the M&A process. Ensure compliance with industry regulations, understand the tax implications, and establish proper contractual agreements to avoid legal or financial issues.

Mergers and acquisitions can significantly impact your LLC, offering opportunities for growth, enhanced capabilities, and entry into new markets. With careful planning, thorough due diligence, and expert guidance, your LLC can use M&A to expand and achieve remarkable business results.

7.3 INNOVATIVE MARKETING STRATEGIES FOR LLC EXPANSION

In today's competitive marketplace, making your business stand out is crucial. Digital marketing plays a vital role in this effort, spotlighting your brand. Search engine optimization (SEO) ensures your business appears first when potential customers search online. SEO revolves around keywords that guide customers to your site. For example, if you sell eco-friendly yoga mats, you want your site to appear first when people search for "eco-friendly yoga gear, "which involves optimizing your website's content and structure, which can be challenging but rewarding.

Next is pay-per-click (PPC) advertising, where you pay for visits to your site. Every time someone clicks on your ad, you pay a fee, but the goal is for those clicks to convert into sales. PPC allows you to target specific demographics. For instance, if you sell trendy sneakers, you can target ads to sneaker enthusiasts.

Social media marketing is another essential tool allowing you to engage directly with your audience. Platforms like Twitter, Instagram, and Facebook offer opportunities to build your brand's personality and connect with customers through posts and interactions.

Content marketing and branding are about telling your brand's story. This approach involves creating blogs, videos, and whitepapers that educate, entertain, and engage your audience. For example, a blog post about "10 Ways to Make Your Home Eco-Friendly" can attract an audience interested in your eco-friendly yoga mats. Videos can provide a personal look into your brand, while whitepapers can position your brand as an authority in your field.

Leveraging partnerships and collaborations can also amplify your brand's reach. Co-marketing with another brand allows you to tap into their audience, effectively increasing your visibility. For instance, partnering with a popular taco truck can introduce your artisanal hot sauces to a new crowd. Affiliate programs, where influencers or other businesses promote your products for a commission, can further boost your reach.

Finally, measuring your marketing effectiveness is crucial. Tools like Google Analytics or social media insights help you understand your campaign's performance, showing you what's working and what isn't. This data empowers you to enhance your strategies, make your marketing efforts more effective, and optimize the use of your resources.

With the right strategies—from SEO and PPC to content creation and partnerships—you can establish a solid digital presence and make your brand stand out. Use these tools to grow your business and achieve your marketing goals.

7.4 UTILIZING TECHNOLOGY FOR BUSINESS GROWTH

In today's fast-moving world, adopting cutting-edge technologies isn't just trendy—it's crucial to your LLC's success. Technologies like cloud computing, artificial intelligence (AI), and the Internet of Things (IoT) offer a faster, smoother way to blend the complex ingredients of your business operations.

Cloud computing, for instance, is like having an infinite pantry at your disposal. It allows you to store massive amounts of data without cluttering your physical space. More than just storage, it enables you to access sophisticated software and infrastructure as needed, turning fixed costs into variable ones and scaling as your business grows. Think about the flexibility of accessing your business data from any device, anywhere in the world—it's like having your office in your pocket.

Then there's AI, which can seem like having a genie at your disposal. From automating customer service through chatbots that never sleep to analyzing data to predict market trends, AI can perform tasks at a scale and speed that humans simply can't match. It's about doing more with less, anticipating your customer's next move before they know it themselves, and personalizing their experience so they feel like your business truly understands their needs.

The Internet of Things (IoT) extends this connectivity to the physical objects in your business environment. For example, sensors in a retail store can track inventory in real time, automatically signaling when stocks are low or when a particular item is flying off the shelves. It's like having eyes and ears in every corner of your business, ensuring you stay connected and responsive.

If you want to expand your business online, your strategy needs to be as robust as your ambition. Choosing the right e-commerce platform is like picking a location for a brick-and-mortar store—it must be accessible, suitable, and advantageous. Whether it's Shopify for its user-friendly interface or Magento for its customization capabilities, your choice should align with your business size, technical ability, and long-term goals.

Optimizing the online customer journey then becomes your next focus. It's about making the path from homepage to checkout as smooth and intuitive as possible. Achieving this might involve streamlining navigation, speeding up page load times, or providing clear, compelling product descriptions. These elements work together to create a seamless shopping experience that draws customers in and keeps them returning.

Cybersecurity is the watchdog of this digital domain. Protecting your business from cyber threats is paramount as you move more of your operations online. Ensuring security means investing in robust and reliable measures like encryption, secure payment gateways, and regular security audits to keep customer data and trust intact.

The mobile arena is another frontier for growth. Mobile optimization is no longer optional, with more people browsing and buying via smartphones. It's about ensuring your website looks as good on a six-inch screen as on a desktop. Responsive design, which automatically adjusts content to fit different screen sizes, is critical here. Additionally, developing a mobile app can enhance the customer experience by offering features like push notifications and offline access, keeping your business at their fingertips.

Finally, we have the technology to enhance customer engagement. Personalized marketing, powered by data analytics and AI, allows you to tailor your marketing messages to individual preferences and behaviors. It's like greeting a returning customer by name and remembering their favorite order—it makes them feel valued and understood. CRM systems efficiently manage these relationships, ensuring you never overlook a customer interaction and seize every opportunity to delight them.

In the grand tapestry of business growth, technology is the thread that connects various elements, weaving them into a cohesive strategy that supports existing operations and drives expansion. From cloud computing and AI to e-commerce and mobile optimization, each technological advancement you adopt can significantly enhance your business's efficiency, scalability, and connectivity. As you integrate these technologies, remember that they are tools to help you build, expand, and connect in ways that were unimaginable just a decade ago. So, embrace them and let them propel your business towards new heights of success.

Reflecting on the transformative power of technology in scaling and evolving your business, we recognize its significant impact. Our journey will continue to explore compliance and legal considerations as we look ahead to ensure that as your business grows, it remains secure, compliant, and prepared for future success.

The Complete LLC Guide For Beginners

Compliance Strategies

* * *

T.J. Griffin

8

COMPLIANCE AND LEGAL ISSUES

Ensuring compliance and handling legalities is essential for your LLC. Each document and report you file is crucial in maintaining your business's smooth operation. Missing a step can lead to significant issues, including audits and regulatory actions. This chapter provides a detailed guide on annual filings and compliance checklists to help your LLC remain secure and prosperous.

8.1 ANNUAL FILINGS AND COMPLIANCE CHECKLISTS FOR LLCS

Understanding Annual Filing Requirements

Annual filings – the paperwork party no business owner can escape. Think of them like your LLC's yearly check-up. Depending on your state, your LLC might need to submit annual reports, pay franchise taxes, or both. These aren't just bureaucratic busywork; they keep your company in good standing.

Failure to comply with legal requirements can lead to severe consequences, including penalties, fines, or even the administrative dissolution of your LLC. For instance, states like Delaware require annual franchise taxes based on the type of company and the number of shares it holds. Meanwhile, states like Missouri demand a yearly report detailing your company's current status and operations. Missing these deadlines can be costly and detrimental to your business, highlighting the importance of staying on top of compliance requirements.

Creating a Compliance Checklist

Let's craft a compliance checklist to avoid the chaos of missed deadlines and frantic last-minute filings. Start by marking all critical filing dates on your calendar – Include tax obligations, reporting deadlines, and any other regulatory submissions specific to your state.

Enhance your compliance checklist by setting reminders a few weeks in advance. These reminders will give you ample time to gather information and prepare documents. Tools like Google Calendar or dedicated business compliance software can provide timely reminders. This proactive approach ensures your LLC remains compliant and helps you avoid penalties, ensuring much smoother operations for your business.

Utilizing Professional Help

Even the most experienced business owners need reliable support, and when it comes to navigating the complexities of legal and tax compliance, a professional can be invaluable. Accountants and compliance specialists are like trusted advisors in the world of bureaucracy. They have the expertise to ensure your business meets all its legal obligations and operates smoothly.

Engaging a professional ensures accuracy in your filings and keeps you updated on any changes in legislation that might affect your business. Think of them as your lookout in the crow's nest, keeping an eye on the horizon for changes in the legal landscape. Whether it's new tax laws or modifications in filing procedures, having a professional on board allows you to focus more on steering your business and less on fretting over paperwork.

Case Examples

There's the story of a small tech startup in Texas that almost lost its right to do business due to a missed annual report. Thankfully, they enlisted the help of a compliance specialist early on, who caught the oversight quickly and helped steer the company back on course before any severe damage was done.

Navigating the complex requirements of LLC compliance might seem daunting, but with a solid plan, a good checklist, and professional assistance, you can keep your business on the right side of the law. Set your schedules, mark your calendars, and ensure your company remains compliant. Here's to smooth operations and successful ventures ahead!

8.2 HANDLING LEGAL DISPUTES: TIPS FOR LLC OWNERS

Legal disputes are a common challenge for LLC owners, but the right strategies can manage them effectively.

Preventive Legal Strategies

First up **prevention**. It's always better to stop disputes before they start. Think of it as putting up a "Beware of the Dog" sign to deter burglaries. Clear contract terms are your first line of defense. When drafting contracts, clarity is king. Ensure that every agreement you enter specifies the rights and obligations of all parties involved as clearly as possible—no surprises, no disputes.

Proper employee training is another crucial preventive measure. Ensure your team understands their job roles and the legal do's and don'ts related to their work, including training on compliance issues, workplace discrimination laws, or your company's internal dispute resolution processes.

Consistent policy enforcement is the thread that ties all your preventive strategies together. It's one thing to have rules but another to apply them consistently. Consistency shows that you mean business and provides a stable framework within which everyone operates.

Resolving Disputes Internally

Despite your best efforts, disputes might still arise, and when they do, resolving them is your next best step. Internal resolution is like settling an argument over board game rules without ruining game night. Mediation techniques can be invaluable here. Appoint an impartial mediator from within your organization, or hire an external professional to help mediate disputes. This approach is less about winning or losing and more about finding a middle ground, ensuring all parties feel heard and valued.

Conflict resolution policies should be clear and accessible to all employees. They should act as a roadmap for handling disputes and outline the steps to take when conflicts arise. It's like having a fire escape plan—everyone should know where and how to use it in an emergency.

Engaging in Formal Dispute Resolution

Despite your best efforts, arbitration and litigation sometimes need a more formal resolution. Arbitration is like having a private judge who listens to both sides and then makes a decision. It's usually faster and less formal than going to court, and it can be binding or non-binding, depending on the terms agreed upon by the parties involved; on the other litigation, taking the dispute to court and having a judge (and possibly a jury) decide the outcome. It's public, usually more costly, and can take a long time to resolve. Think of it as taking our dinner party dispute to a televised debate—it's a big deal, and everyone will know about it.

Documenting Dispute Resolution

Last but certainly not least, document every step taken during the dispute resolution process. Keeping a clear record is crucial, Whether mediation, arbitration, or litigation. It's like keeping a detailed diary of events. Documentation can provide invaluable evidence if the dispute escalates further and help you refine your dispute resolution processes.

Handling legal disputes might not be the most fun part of running an LLC, but you can confidently navigate these tricky waters with the right strategies. Think of yourself as the ship's captain steering through a storm—stay calm, use your tools, and keep your crew informed. With preventive strategies, internal resolution processes, and options for formal resolution, you're well-equipped to handle any disputes.

8.3 UPDATING YOUR LLC DOCUMENTATION: WHEN AND HOW

Keeping your LLC's documentation updated is crucial as your business evolves to reflect changes in your business structure, operations, or state laws. Regularly reviewing and updating your documents ensures that your LLC remains compliant and accurately represents your current business reality.

What are the signs that your LLC's documents need a refresh? Changes in LLC membership are a glaring signal. If members have come or gone or ownership percentages have shifted, your operating agreement needs to reflect these changes accurately. Similarly, significant shifts in business operations—like adding a new product line or expanding into new states—can alter the liabilities and responsibilities in your foundational documents. Lastly, keep an eye on changes in state law as regulations and legal requirements shift throughout the years. Staying compliant means staying updated.

Updating documents isn't just about crossing out old information and scribbling in the new. It's a systematic process that ensures all members agree with every change legally and unanimously. Start by gathering all LLC members to discuss and approve the changes. This session will allow you to decide which business strategies are in and which are out.

Once you've agreed on the changes, it's time to document them. Amend your operating agreement, articles of organization, or any other affected official documents, which might involve drafting new sections or rewriting existing ones to reflect the current state of affairs better.

The next step is filing these amendments with the relevant state agencies. Depending on where your LLC is registered, you may need to submit forms detailing the changes and a filing fee. Ensure you know your state's specific filing requirements to avoid legal issues.

Keeping your LLC's documentation up-to-date is more than just a bureaucratic chore; it's a legal necessity that can have significant implications. Outdated documents can lead to members' disputes over roles and responsibilities. It's like relying on an old map while the roads have changed—confusion and conflict are almost guaranteed. Moreover, compliance with state laws is not optional. Operating with outdated documents can lead to penalties, fines, or even the loss of your LLC's good standing with the state.

Establish a regular review schedule to ensure your LLC's documents are always in season. How often should this happen? It's a good practice to review your LLC's status annually, aligning it with other routine business evaluations like your annual financial review or tax filings. This regular check-up enables you to identify and address any necessary changes, ensuring your LLC remains legally compliant and up to date with current regulations.

Think of your LLC as a living entity that grows and evolves. Its documents are not just paperwork but reflect its current structure and strategy. Keeping these documents updated is akin to keeping your business narrative clear and your operations smooth. So, dust off those files, gather your LLC members, and get those documents tailored to fit your business today, ready to meet tomorrow's challenges.

8.4 THE CONSEQUENCES OF NON-COMPLIANCE FOR LLCS

Complying with state and federal regulations is essential. Non-compliance can lead to severe consequences, making your business stand out for the wrong reasons. Let's explore the critical aspects of compliance and the potential repercussions when your LLC fails to meet these requirements.

State Penalties and Fees

Each state has its own set of rules. If your LLC fails to comply with these rules, the penalties can range from a slap on the wrist to a full-blown shutdown of your business operations. For instance, timely filings can lead to late fees accumulating quickly and potentially growing into significant debts that threaten your business's financial health.

Then there's the biggie—operational penalties. Imagine this: you forget to renew your LLC registration, and the state suspends your authority to operate. You'll need to pay fines, sometimes including back taxes with interest. If you neglect this for too long in some states, the authorities could involuntarily dissolve your LLC. Poof! Just like that, your business is no more. Are you reinstating an LLC after dissolution? Now, that's a costly and complex comeback tour that no business owner wants to headline.

Federal Consequences

Failing to meet your tax obligations can result in severe penalties from the IRS, which can be much more substantial than state penalties. These penalties aren't just about paying what you owe; late payments can accrue interest, turning a manageable bill into significant debt.

The financial impact is only part of the issue. Federal non-compliance can trigger audits, where authorities examine your financial records. If they find discrepancies during an audit, you could face legal sanctions, additional fines, or, in extreme cases, criminal charges. Such consequences can threaten your business's survival and your freedom. Therefore, maintaining compliance is essential to avoid these severe repercussions.

Impact on Business Reputation

The ripple effects of non-compliance don't stop at your wallet. They extend to your business's reputation. In our hyper-connected world, news travels fast, and the news of your LLC's non-compliance could spread even faster. Clients, investors, and partners are unlikely to trust a business that can't keep its legal affairs in order.

This reputational damage can be particularly devastating if you're in an industry where trust is everything, like financial services or health care. You should invest heavily in PR and marketing to counteract the negative press.

Reinstating Compliance

If you miss a compliance requirement, you can correct it promptly and carefully. Federal authorities will scrutinize your financial records if you don't follow the rules and guidelines. You will face legal sanctions, additional fines, or criminal charges if they find discrepancies in the most severe cases. These penalties can jeopardize your business's viability and your freedom. Thus, staying compliant is crucial to prevent these significant consequences.

Taking these steps can help get your business back on track.

Next, contact the necessary agencies, both state and federal. Open communication can sometimes mitigate penalties, especially if you're proactive and committed to resolving the issues. Make sure you show that you're serious about getting it right.

Sometimes, the process is overwhelming, or the stakes are too high to handle alone. In such cases, roping in professionals—lawyers, accountants, or compliance specialists—can be a game-changer. They can navigate the complex legal landscape, negotiate with authorities on your behalf, and help set up systems to prevent future slip-ups.

Non-compliance can significantly impact your LLC, but you can resolve these issues with a clear understanding of the consequences and a solid plan to address them. Staying aligned with legal and regulatory requirements keeps you out of trouble, enhances your business's credibility, and sets a strong foundation for long-term success.

The key to a smooth performance is preparation, awareness, and quick action when things go awry. Keep your business practices in harmony with legal requirements, and you'll set the stage for ongoing success, free from the dissonance of legal troubles. Next, we'll explore financing options for your LLC, ensuring you have the capital to grow and thrive in the competitive business arena.

∼

The Complete LLC Guide For Beginners

Finance Options, Tax Benefits & Future-Proofing Your LLC

* * *

T.J. Griffin

9

FINANCING YOUR LLC

Financing your LLC can be approached in various ways, each with unique advantages. One common strategy is bootstrapping, which involves using your resources to grow your business. Instead of relying on external funding, you leverage what you already have to build and expand your company. This method allows you to maintain control and minimize debt, making it a popular choice for many entrepreneurs.

9.1 BOOTSTRAPPING YOUR LLC: STRATEGIES FOR SELF-FUNDING

Understanding Bootstrapping

Bootstrapping is the art of funding your business without turning to outside help. It's about pulling yourself up by your bootstraps, quite literally. In the entrepreneurial sense, it means relying on your savings, revenue, and sheer grit to power your business engine. Why is this significant? It keeps you in the driver's seat. Without external investors, you call the shots, which means you can steer your business exactly where you want it to go without backseat drivers offering their two cents on every decision.

This method is not just about maintaining control; it's also about minimizing debt. By funding your operations from your pocket, you avoid the shackles of high-interest loans or the pressure of pleasing investors. Bootstrapping is perfect for those who prefer to start small and grow organically, ensuring that the foundation of the business is solid and dependable.

Effective Bootstrapping Techniques

How can you bootstrap effectively? Start by reducing unnecessary expenses. This strategy means something other than compromising on quality or essentials but becoming skilled at budgeting and cost-cutting. Negotiate for the best deals on everything from office supplies to service contracts, and reinvest every penny saved back into your business.

Reinvesting profits is another cornerstone of bootstrapping. Instead of using your initial earnings for non-essential purchases, reinvest them into the business. This reinvestment can accelerate growth and increase profits, creating a self-sustaining cycle.

Another key tactic is optimizing operational efficiency. Streamline your processes, automate where possible, and always look for ways to increase productivity without increasing costs. By improving efficiency, you can achieve more with the same resources and help your business grow sustainably.

Advantages and Challenges

Like all good things, bootstrapping comes with its own set of challenges and advantages. On the plus side, as mentioned, you retain complete control and reduce debt. These benefits allow quicker decision-making capabilities—you can pivot, twist, and turn without having to file a motion with a board or plead your case to investors. It's entrepreneurial freedom at its best.

Bootstrapping can mean slower growth. Without a significant injection of capital, scaling up takes longer. It's a marathon, not a sprint, requiring patience and endurance. There's also personal risk. Since you're using your funds, it can affect your financial health if the business fails. It's like betting on a horse race; the rewards can be great, but risk's always involved.

Real-Life Examples

Let's spotlight some bootstrapping success stories to paint a clearer picture. Consider the tale of a tech startup that began in a college dorm room. The founders used their savings to buy second-hand computers and spent months coding their software. They slowly but surely expanded by reinvesting every dime from early sales into the business. Today, they're a leading software provider, all without a penny of outside funding.

Then there's the story of a boutique bakery that started with one mixer and a lot of passion. The owner used her savings to lease a small space and worked 16-hour days crafting and selling her creations. As her reputation grew, so did her profits, which she reinvested in better equipment and marketing. Now, she owns a chain of cafes across the state, a testament to the power of bootstrapping.

As you consider financing options for your LLC, remember that bootstrapping is just one method to get your business off the ground. It requires grit, determination, and a keen sense of management. But for those who pull it off, it can lead to financial success and a profound sense of accomplishment. You built this. Now, let's see how you can make it grow.

9.2 SECURING LOANS AND LINES OF CREDIT: A GUIDE FOR LLCS

Sometimes, your funds might not be enough to support your LLC's growth. In such cases, loans and lines of credit can provide the necessary financial support. Think of these as a way to refuel your business and keep moving towards your goals. Before you proceed, it's essential to understand the different types of financing available and how to use them wisely.

Traditional business loans are reliable and secure financing options. Banks offer various loan types to meet business needs, such as purchasing new equipment or expanding premises. The advantages include lower interest rates and longer repayment terms, which can help manage your cash flow. However, these loans often require extensive documentation and collateral, and getting approval can be challenging but achievable.

U.S. Small Business Administration (SBA) loans. Think of these as your business's scholarship program. The SBA loans help small businesses that might not qualify for traditional loans get the needed funding. SBA loans are backed by government guarantees, which can make them less risky for lenders and more accessible for you. However, the application process can be as detailed and lengthy as a doctoral thesis.

Lines of credit are another great tool in your financial toolkit. Picture this as your credit card but for your LLC. They offer flexibility because you only draw what you need when needed, making it ideal for managing cash flow or unexpected expenses. The advantage? You pay interest only on the amount you use. The downside? Higher interest rates than traditional loans and the temptation to overuse them can put you in a tricky financial spot.

Preparing to Apply for a Loan

Applying for a loan requires thorough preparation. Building a solid business credit score is like your training regime. Pay your bills on time, reduce your debt levels, and keep your credit lines open, but use them wisely. Lenders look at your business credit score to gauge your reliability. Think of it as your financial fitness level—the higher it is, the more attractive you are to lenders.

Crafting a compelling business plan is your race strategy. It should map out your business model, market analysis, financial projections, and the unique selling points of your LLC. This plan doesn't just show lenders where you're going; it shows them you have a clear path to get there and a strategy to overcome potential hurdles.

Gathering the necessary financial documents ready will help speed up the loan process. Ensure you have at least two years of organized and available financial statements, tax returns, and bank statements. These documents are proof of your business's economic health and operational history.

Navigating the Application Process

Stepping into the loan application process can feel like entering a maze. Each lender has its pathways and pitfalls. To boost your chances of finishing, start with a clear understanding of the loan terms. Be sure to ask your lender for a cost estimate to give you a clear picture of the overall loan numbers, such as interest rate, repayment schedule, fees, and monthly payments.

Personal relationships can also play a pivotal role. If you have a good relationship with your bank or lender, don't hesitate to leverage it. A familiar face can often make the process smoother and faster.

Finally, transparency is crucial. Be honest about your business's strengths and weaknesses. Lenders appreciate honesty and are more willing to work with you if they feel they're getting the complete picture.

Managing Loan Repayments

Effectively managing your loan repayments is essential for maintaining financial health and building a positive relationship with your lender. Establishing a budget for regular payments helps keep your finances in order and ensures you don't strain your cash flow.

Ask your lender if your loan has a prepayment penalty clause. While paying off your loan early can save you on interest, some lenders charge penalties for early repayment.

Navigating the world of loans and lines of credit can be daunting, but with the proper preparation and understanding, you can fuel your LLC's growth effectively and sustainably. Remember, the key to securing a loan is thorough preparation and transparency to ensure a successful outcome.

9.3 ATTRACTING INVESTORS: PITCHING YOUR LLC SUCCESSFULLY

Making the right first impression is crucial when attracting investors for your LLC. It's all about presenting yourself effectively and nurturing the connection to build a fruitful relationship.

The first step? Identifying potential investors who aren't just looking for a quick profit but are genuinely interested in what your business stands for and plans to achieve.

Look for individuals or entities that align with your industry, show interest in your business size and stage, and have a history of investing in similar business models. This could mean scouring industry reports, attending networking events, or joining online platforms connecting startups with investors. Remember, the goal here isn't just to find any investor; it's to find the right investor who resonates with your business vision and growth plans.

Once you've spotted potential investors, crafting an effective pitch is your next crucial step. Start by clearly articulating your LLC's value proposition. What makes your business stand out? Why is your product or service the next big thing? Be concise but compelling. Next, outline the market potential. Investors need to see that the market is big enough for your business to survive and thrive. Show them the numbers and trends that support your business case.

The return on investment (ROI): Use forecasts and financial models to paint a picture of how and when they can expect to see returns. Be realistic but optimistic. Avoid fluffy jargon and stick to the facts and figures underlying your business's potential profitability. This part of your pitch needs to be tight; ambiguity or over-optimism can be a turn-off.

Negotiating investment terms is tricky but very doable; you need to know what you're willing to offer and where you draw the line. This process involves equity distribution, voting rights, and exit strategies. How much of your company are you willing to give up? What decision-making powers will the investors have? And, importantly, what's the exit plan? Whether it's a buy-back agreement, an IPO (Initial Public Offering), or a sale, having clear terms laid out can prevent many headaches. This step is crucial in maintaining a healthy relationship with your investors—it sets clear expectations and provides a roadmap for the partnership.

Finally, let's talk about the legal stuff. Bringing on investors is not just a handshake deal; securities laws bind it and require formal agreements. Compliance with securities laws is critical; you don't want the SEC knocking on your door. Ensuring proper documentation of your investment offering is essential, which might include a private placement memorandum if you're dealing with private investors or registration with the SEC if you're going public. Every document should be watertight, from the terms of investment to the rights and responsibilities of each party involved.

Consider working with a lawyer specializing in securities and investment law to ensure everything is up and up. They can help you navigate the complexities of investment laws, draft the necessary documents, and ensure that your interests and those of your investors are legally protected.

Attracting and securing the right investors for your LLC can be a game-changer. It's about more than just getting funds; it's about building partnerships that propel your business forward. With the right approach, you can turn potential investors from mere acquaintances in a coffee shop into crucial allies in your entrepreneurial adventure. So, tune your pitch, understand your worth, negotiate wisely, and always keep it legal.

9.4 CROWDFUNDING OPPORTUNITIES FOR LLCS: A MODERN APPROACH TO FUNDING

In the digital age, crowdfunding has emerged as the cool kid on the block in finance. It's like throwing a massive online party where guests bring cash instead of gifts to help kickstart your business dreams into reality. Crowdfunding comes in several flavors, each with its charm. First, there's *reward-based crowdfunding*, akin to pre-selling your product. You might offer early bird specials or exclusive perks as a thank-you to your backers. Then there's *equity-based crowdfunding*, where backers get a slice of the equity pie, making them mini-stakeholders in your venture. And let's not forget *debt-based crowdfunding*, where folks lend you money, and you pay it back with interest over time, much like a traditional loan.

Planning your crowdfunding campaign requires careful preparation and execution. Start by setting realistic financial goals and determining how much you need to raise to make your project successful, but keep your target achievable. Craft your story to connect emotionally with potential backers by sharing your journey, the passion behind your project, and the impact their support will have. Make your story personal, compelling, and honest.

Here is how to choose the right platform that aligns with your project type and audience preferences—Each crowdfunding platform has its audience and niche. Kickstarter might be great for creative projects, Indiegogo offers more flexibility with funding rules, and GoFundMe could be ideal for personal or charitable causes. Pick one that aligns with your project type and audience preferences. The platform will take a cut of your funds, so factor that into your financial planning.

Engaging with backers is where the magic happens. It's not just about getting their money; it's about building relationships. Update your backers regularly about the project's progress. Did you hit a milestone? Share it! Have you encountered a setback? Be transparent about it. This ongoing dialogue makes backers feel involved and valued, turning them from mere contributors to passionate advocates of your project.

ENGAGING WITH BACKERS: THE HEART OF CROWDFUNDING

Keeping backers in the loop is pivotal. Regular updates, whether through emails, social media posts, or video diaries, keep the momentum and engagement high. It's like giving your audience behind-the-scenes access to a film production. They see the ups, the downs, and everything in between, which builds trust and loyalty.

Transparent communication is your best policy here. If there are delays or challenges, share them openly. Backers appreciate honesty and are often more supportive when understanding your hurdles. And when you hit those big wins, celebrate them with your backers! Let them know their support is making fundamental differences.

Fulfilling promises is crucial. If you promised rewards, deliver them on time and as described. If it's an equity campaign, sort out all the paperwork and legal issues. This approach builds trust and protects your reputation for future business ventures.

Post-Campaign Activities: Keeping the Momentum

Once the campaign wraps up, the work isn't over. Managing the funds responsibly and using the money as promised is essential. Detailed budgeting and transparent accounting are crucial at this stage. Backers should be able to see how you spent every dollar in bringing the project to life.

Delivering on promises is as crucial after the campaign as it is during. If you promise rewards, ensure they are delivered to your backers as pledged. Quality control is critical here; the last thing you want is for backers to feel disappointed with the fruits of their investment.

Maintaining relationships with backers after the campaign can turn one-time supporters into lifelong fans. Keep them updated with post-campaign progress, offer exclusive insights, and consider them first for future products or releases. It's about turning that initial support into a lasting community.

Crowdfunding isn't just a funding mechanism; it's a community-building tool. When done right, it provides the capital to launch your project and creates a tribe of supporters who believe in your vision and invest fully in your success. As you wrap up this chapter, remember that successful crowdfunding is as much about building relationships as it is about raising funds. With a compelling story, engaged backers, and a clear fulfillment plan, your crowdfunding campaign can be more than just a fundraiser—it can be the launchpad for a thriving community around your LLC.

10

ADVANCED TAX STRATEGIES

This section guides you to uncover valuable tax deductions and credits available to LLCs. Understanding these tax benefits allows you to make informed decisions that help your business save money and enhance profitability. Let's explore the tax code to find opportunities to improve your LLC's financial health significantly.

10.1 ADVANCED TAX DEDUCTIONS AND CREDITS FOR LLCS

Identifying Lesser-Known Deductions

Diving into the world of tax deductions can feel like exploring a jungle—lush with potential savings yet dense and easy to get lost in. Beyond the standard deductions like office supplies and travel expenses, a thicket of lesser-known deductions could make a substantial difference to your tax bill. For instance, did you know upgrading your office to be more energy-efficient is good for the planet and your pocket? Yep, energy-efficient appliances or systems can snag you some sweet deductions.

Then there are deductions specific to your industry—for example, if you're in the manufacturing sector, you might be able to deduct costs associated with particular productions or research activities. The key here is to keep a keen eye on what's unique about your business operations and to consult with a tax professional who can help you spot these hidden gems.

Maximizing Credits

Let's move on from deductions to credits, which can be even more lucrative for your LLC because they reduce your tax bill dollar-for-dollar. For instance, the R&D tax credit rewards businesses for engaging in research and development in the U.S. It's like finding a giant pearl in an oyster—potentially very valuable. Still, you need to dive deep to see it.

To maximize these credits, you need to know they exist, understand how to qualify for them, and claim them correctly. Each credit has its own set of rules and qualifications, and navigating them can be akin to decoding a complex ancient script. Whether it's the Disabled Access Credit for making your business more accessible or the Work Opportunity Tax Credit for hiring from certain demographic groups, these credits have specific requirements you must meet to benefit.

Documentation and Tracking

Claiming these deductions and credits is no small feat and requires rigorous documentation and tracking. Solid records must back up every expense you deduct and every credit you claim, which means keeping receipts, detailed accounts, and even logs of activities (like research and development efforts).

Good documentation practices are not just about compliance; they are your best defense in the stormy seas of tax audits. If the IRS ever questions your claims, your well-kept records are your armor and shield, proving that you've played by the rules. It's tedious, yes, but it's also imperative.

Case Studies on Effective Use

Consider the case of a tech startup that utilized the R&D tax credit to offset the cost of developing a new app. By meticulously documenting their development process, employee contributions, and project expenses, they could claim a significant tax credit, which bolstered their cash flow during the critical early stages of their business.

Take the example of a small cafe that invested in energy-efficient appliances and received not only a deduction for the expenses but also a tax credit for the energy efficiency improvements. The savings from these tax benefits allowed the cafe to expand its seating area, thus increasing its revenue. Understanding and applying the right tax strategies turned potential expenditures into profitable investments.

As we continue to explore the vast benefits of tax strategies available for LLCs, remember that each decision you make, the deduction you claim, and the credit you pursue is a step towards optimizing your business's financial health. Keep your documents organized, consult with your tax professionals, and always watch for hidden gems in the tax code.

10.2 HANDLING MULTI-STATE TAXATION FOR EXPANDING LLCS

Understanding Nexus Rules

Navigating multi-state taxation for LLCs can be complex, as each state has unique tax obligations. Like accommodating various dietary preferences at a large gathering, you must address different tax requirements, from standard business taxes to specialized obligations in every state. The term 'nexus' in tax terminology refers to a connection or presence sufficient in a state to obligate your LLC to comply with its tax regulations. Examples of such connections include having a physical store, employing workers, or storing inventory in a state.

Recent shifts like the boom in online sales and the rise of remote work have stretched the traditional boundaries of nexus. States are keener than ever to get their share of the tax pie from businesses operating without a brick-and-mortar presence in their borders. Take South Dakota v. Wayfair, Inc., a landmark Supreme Court case that changed the old nexus rules by allowing states to charge tax on sales from out-of-state sellers. No physical presence? That is no problem, according to the new regulations. If your LLC sells or delivers products across state lines, you might have a tax obligation in states you've never set foot in.

Navigating these waters requires a keen understanding of each state's nexus rules, which can vary as wildly as party snack preferences. Staying informed through constant research or, better yet, consulting with tax professionals who specialize in state tax law can help you avoid unexpected tax bills that could dampen your entrepreneurial spirit.

Navigating Varying State Tax Laws

Handling varying state tax laws is like playing a game where the rules change depending on where you're standing. What works tax-wise in California might not fly in New York. Each state sets its rates and regulations on what constitutes taxable revenue, which forms to file, and when those dreaded deadlines hit. It's a juggling act that requires precision and planning.

One effective strategy is to use specialized multi-state tax software. These digital wizards can help you track sales and tax rates across different states, automate tax filings, and even update you on regulatory changes. It's like having a GPS that shows the fastest route and warns you about speed traps and road closures (a.k.a. tax audits and law changes).

Another smart move is building a relationship with regional tax experts. These pros are like local guides who know the lay of the land. They can provide insights into specific state tax climates and help tailor your tax strategies accordingly. Whether it's navigating California's complex sales tax laws or capitalizing on Texas's absence of state income tax, these experts can offer tailored advice that could save your LLC significant money and headaches.

Apportionment Strategies for Business Income

When apportioning income among different states, think of it as slicing a pie. Just as you decide how to cut the pie based on the size and appetite of your guests, you need to determine how much of your LLC's income belongs to each state where you operate. This decision is crucial because it affects how much tax you'll pay to each state.

Most states use a formula that considers the percentage of your sales, payroll, and property within the state. If you have 50% of your sales, 30% of your payroll, and 20% of your property in State X, then a significant chunk of your income might be taxable there. Getting this mix right is more art than science, often requiring simulations and projections to find the most tax-efficient strategy.

Always consider the implications of these apportionment strategies on your overall tax liability. Missteps here can lead to double taxation or hefty fines for underpayment. Regular reviews and adjustments to your plan, guided by detailed financial data and expert advice, are your best bet for keeping your tax obligations in check without dampening your business growth.

Avoiding Common Pitfalls

Finally, let's talk about avoiding the common pitfalls of multi-state taxation. The most frequent blunders include failing to register for tax in a state where you have nexus, missing filing deadlines, and double taxation due to poor apportionment planning. These mistakes can lead to penalties and interest and damage your LLC's compliance record, making it harder to operate smoothly across state lines.

Proactive planning is critical. Set up systems and reminders for tax deadlines and regularly review your nexus status in each state. Consider conducting annual or bi-annual reviews of your tax strategy with the help of your regional tax experts. They can help you spot potential risks and take corrective actions before they become costly problems.

Navigating the maze of multi-state taxation is no small feat. Still, with careful planning, the right tools, and expert guidance, you can ensure that your expanding LLC remains compliant and financially healthy across all state lines. Remember, in multi-state operations, being well-prepared is not just good practice; it's a necessity.

10.3 TAX PLANNING: PREPARING FOR YEAR-END TAX OBLIGATIONS

The end of the year is a perfect time for festive cheer, holiday shopping, and strategic tax planning to save your LLC money. Year-end tax planning is essential for optimizing your financial situation. Just as you wouldn't skip decorating for the holidays, you should only let the year close by optimizing your tax position. Let's explore some intelligent tax strategies to help you keep more money in your pocket.

Year-End Tax Moves

First up on our list are the year-end tax moves. One classic strategy is deferring income. Now, this sounds like you're just delaying the inevitable, but by pushing income into the following year, you can lower your tax bill this year. This modification could be especially beneficial if you anticipate being in a lower tax bracket next year due to changed circumstances or planned income reductions.

Accelerating deductions is another festive trick. If you've had a high-income year, bumping your deductible expenses before the year ends can reduce your taxable income. This shift could involve making those office upgrades you've been considering or stocking up on supplies. It's akin to buying all your holiday gifts early to take advantage of a massive sale.

Lastly, consider making last-minute purchases or investments the company can write off. These actions help reduce your tax liability and position your business better for the coming year. It's like upgrading your holiday lights to energy-efficient LEDs; initially, it's a cost, but the savings light up over time.

Estimating Tax Payments

Accurately estimating your tax payments is crucial to avoid the January blues—underpayment penalties. The IRS isn't too jolly if they find you've paid less than you owe. Use the IRS-provided worksheets and tools like the *Estimated Tax Worksheet to stay on their nice list*. It helps you calculate how much you should be paying each quarter. Using accounting software to keep track of your income and deductions throughout the year can also make this task easier. Think of it as holding a naughty or nice list for your finances; it helps when it's time to report to the IRS.

Leveraging Retirement Plans

Contributing to a retirement plan like an IRA or a 401(k) isn't just a wise move for your future self's leisure years; it's also a fantastic tax deferral tactic. These contributions can reduce your taxable income now while securing your golden years. Plus, many retirement plans offer tax-deferred growth, meaning you will only pay taxes on the earnings once you withdraw them. It's like spending holiday money in a piggy bank that grows over time without the taxman dipping into it yearly.

Charitable Contributions

Donating to charity feels good and looks good on your tax return. You can write off contributions to qualified charities, lowering your taxable income. However, the key here is documentation. Ensure you keep detailed records of all donations, including receipts and acknowledgment letters from the charities. If the IRS questions your deductions, proper documentation ensures you have the proof ready.

So, there you have it: a festive guide to wrapping up your fiscal year with a bow. By making smart moves now, you can ensure that when the ball drops on New Year's Eve, you're celebrating the start of a new year and your financial savvy, which will pay dividends in the coming year. Cheers to that!

10.4 LEVERAGING TAX PROFESSIONALS: WHEN YOU SHOULD HIRE AN EXPERT

Navigating the tax seas can sometimes feel like steering a ship through a storm, especially when complex tax issues arise or the dreaded audit looms. In times like these, you might wish for a seasoned navigator, a.k.a. a tax professional, who can take the wheel and guide you safely to shore. Recognizing when to bring such an expert on board is crucial. For instance, if you're facing an audit, you'll want someone who knows the rules and can speak the language fluently. Similarly, the tax implications can be pretty complex if you plan significant business changes—like expanding interstate or drastically altering your business model. A tax pro can help you align all the numbers correctly.

Choosing the right tax professional is akin to selecting a crew member for your ship. You need someone who knows their way around a tax form and understands the nuances of your particular industry. Start by looking for a tax advisor with experience with LLCs who is familiar with your sector's specific challenges and opportunities. Whether you're a tech startup or a boutique retail chain, different industries have different tax landscapes. A savvy advisor who's navigated similar waters before can provide insights and strategies tailored to your unique needs. And don't forget to check their credentials and client testimonials to ensure their reliability and trustworthiness.

Bringing an expert on board costs money, but the right tax advisor can ensure compliance and identify tax savings and strategies that far outweigh their fees. They can help you avoid costly mistakes and penalties and maximize your tax returns. It's about spending a little now to save a lot later, securing both peace of mind and a more favorable financial outcome.

Building a Relationship with Your Tax Advisor

Fostering a robust and productive relationship with your tax advisor is like cultivating a fruitful partnership with a trusted first mate. Communication is key. Be transparent about your business operations, financial goals, and any concerns. Regular meetings are essential—not just at tax time but throughout the year—to discuss changes in your business and emerging tax issues. This ongoing dialogue ensures that your advisor understands your business in-depth and can provide tailored advice.

Effective use of their services goes beyond mere compliance. Involve your tax professional in strategic planning, especially when considering new ventures or adjustments to your business model. Their insights can help you evaluate potential decisions' financial viability and tax implications. Consider your tax advisor a strategic ally who can help navigate tax waters and broader financial seas.

While taxes might seem daunting, they must not be a solo journey. With the right tax professional, you can confidently navigate even the most challenging fiscal waters, ensuring your LLC remains compliant and thrives.

11

ADAPTING TO CHANGES AND FUTURE-PROOFING YOUR LLC

Running a business involves maintaining balance, anticipating changes, and adjusting accordingly. This chapter focuses on strategies to keep your LLC ahead, ensuring it remains resilient and prosperous in the face of future challenges.

11.1 ANTICIPATING MARKET TRENDS. HOW TO KEEP YOUR LLC COMPETITIVE

Staying ahead of market trends isn't just brilliant; it's essential. But how do you spot these trends? Well, you don't need a crystal ball. You need the right tools and a keen eye.

Identifying Emerging Trends

Tools like Google Trends, social media analytics, and industry reports provide a comprehensive view of current trends. However, it's not just about observing; it's also about engaging. Participate in industry forums, subscribe to leading industry journals, and monitor your competitors. Attention to these sources will give you valuable insights into market movements and opportunities.

Adapting your business strategies to these insights is essential to your LLC. Say you run a boutique and notice a rising trend sustainably. It's not enough to just stock up on eco-friendly fabrics. You might need to rethink your marketing strategies to highlight sustainability or adjust your supply chains to favor green suppliers. It's like seeing storm clouds gather and deciding to sell umbrellas. You're not just predicting rain; you're preparing to make a splash when it pours.

Adapting Business Strategies

Adapting isn't just about survival; it's about thriving. It means sometimes rethinking how you do what you do. Maybe it's diversifying your product lines or tweaking your service delivery methods. For instance, introducing vegan options could be wise if you own a cafe and realize there's a burgeoning demand for plant-based diets. Or perhaps the trend is towards remote work; could you turn part of your cafe into co-working spaces during off-peak hours? It's about being flexible and creative.

Utilizing Competitive Intelligence

Competitive intelligence is about understanding your competitors' strengths and weaknesses and learning from them. Tools like SEMrush can help you analyze competitors' online strategies, and conducting a SWOT analysis can help you understand where you stand in comparison. The more you know about your competitors, the better you can strategize and position your business.

Continuous Learning and Innovation

Fostering a culture of continuous learning and innovation within your LLC is to ensure your business is lined up and ready to go. Encourage your team to stay curious and proactive. Invest in training programs, attend workshops, and set aside time for brainstorming sessions where the idea could be more varied. Remember, Netflix didn't kill Blockbuster. Complacency did. Keep paddling, keep looking for the next wave, and maybe, just maybe, you'll find that you're not just riding the waves but making them.

By staying agile, continuously learning, and keeping your finger on the market's pulse, your LLC won't just survive; it will thrive. Whether leveraging cutting-edge market research tools, adapting to new consumer preferences, or using competitive intelligence, the goal is to keep your business on the leading edge—ready to catch the next big wave of opportunity. So keep your eyes on the horizon; the next big thing could be closer than it appears.

11.2 THE IMPACT OF TECHNOLOGICAL ADVANCES ON YOUR LLC

Let's talk tech, shall we? Think of technology as your LLC's superpower. Whether it's speeding up operations with a flash of automation or connecting with customers across the globe at the click of a button, technology is the secret sauce that can skyrocket your business into the stratosphere. But before you strap on your jetpack, let's figure out how to harness this power effectively.

Evaluating Technological Needs

Assessing your LLC's current tech setup isn't about counting how many gadgets and gizmos you've accumulated over the years; it's about understanding where your tech game stands and where it needs to level up. Start by identifying the bottlenecks in your operations. It could be the glacial pace of data entry or the chaotic symphony of an uncoordinated team. Whatever it is, pinpointing these pain points can highlight where technology can make a real difference.

Conducting a thorough audit of your existing systems to identify technological deficits holding back your business is essential. Determine whether your systems are integrated or isolated and whether they communicate smoothly. This investigation will highlight weaknesses and reveal opportunities for tech-driven solutions that could enhance your business operations.

Integrating New Technologies

Integrating new technologies, such as cloud services, AI tools, or advanced analytics, can seem daunting, but consider setting up a new smartphone. With a bit of setup time, some customization, and voilà, you're ready to play.

Let's say you decide to adopt cloud computing. This approach isn't just about storing files somewhere in the ether; it's about accessing your business operations from anywhere, providing you with a virtual office in your pocket.

The ROI? Increased flexibility, enhanced collaboration, and a significant reduction in IT costs. Or you're eyeing AI tools to personalize customer interactions. Imagine an AI chatbot that doesn't just answer queries but predicts what your customers might ask next. It's like having a mind-reading assistant who's always on duty.

Integrating these technologies should be done with a strategy in mind. It's not about throwing spaghetti at the wall and seeing what sticks. Define clear goals for what you want the tech to achieve, ensure it aligns with your business objectives, and prepare your team for the transition. Training is critical here—make sure everyone's on board and up to speed, or your high-tech sailboat might drift aimlessly.

Cybersecurity Measures

Cybersecurity: As you embrace more technology, the target on your back for cyber threats grows bigger. Protecting your digital assets and sensitive information is no longer optional; it's imperative.

Start with strong passwords, secure networks, and regular software updates. Think of these as the locks and alarms on your digital house.

But don't stop there. Implement more sophisticated measures like multi-factor authentication, encryption, and firewalls. It's like adding a moat and some watchtowers to your fortress.

Regularly training your team on cybersecurity best practices is a priority. After all, the most robust security system can be compromised by a simple human error—like clicking on a phishing link. Make cybersecurity awareness a part of your company culture. It's like having a well-trained guard dog; it might not stop every intruder, but it will make them think twice.

Staying Updated with Tech Developments

The tech landscape changes quickly, and staying updated is the only way to ensure your LLC is relevant.

Subscribe to tech-focused publications, follow thought leaders on social media, or join tech forums. Better yet, attend tech conferences or engage with tech incubators. These can be goldmines of information and networking opportunities. It's like having a backstage pass to the future, giving you insights into emerging technologies that could benefit your business.

Your LLC can survive and thrive in the digital age by staying proactive about technological advances, accurately assessing needs, integrating new technologies wisely, maintaining stringent cybersecurity measures, and keeping informed about ongoing developments. Think of technology as your business's wings; manage it well and watch it soar to new heights.

11.3 LEGISLATIVE CHANGES: STAYING INFORMED AND COMPLIANT

Running an LLC requires staying updated on ever-changing laws and regulations to avoid legal problems. Laws, regulations, and tax codes can change frequently due to new government policies, economic shifts, or societal demands. Staying informed is crucial for ensuring your business remains compliant and successful.

Monitoring Legal Changes

Keeping your business compliant starts with knowing what to comply with. It's like being in a game where the rules keep changing. To avoid being caught off guard, ensure you have reliable sources for updates. Subscribe to legal newsletters, follow regulatory bodies on social media, or use legal update services to stay informed. These resources can send alerts to your inbox or phone, alerting you whenever a significant change might affect your business. Also, consider attending industry conferences and seminars; these can provide valuable insights and a chance to network with others who might have navigated similar changes.

Impact Assessment

Once you know a new law or regulation, the next step is figuring out how it impacts your business operations. Conducting a thorough risk assessment is crucial here. You'll want to gather your team and analyze what these changes mean for your current operations. Are there new procedures to follow? Do your products need to be adjusted? It's like realizing the game has switched from checkers to chess. You need to understand the new rules thoroughly to continue playing effectively.

For instance, if a new environmental regulation affects your production line's waste disposal, map out how this might disrupt your operations or increase your costs. This kind of planning isn't just about preventing negative impacts; it's also about identifying potential opportunities that new regulations might create. Maybe this change will lead you to adopt more sustainable practices to open up a new market of eco-conscious consumers.

Implementing Compliance Changes

Implementing these changes in your business is all about action. Suppose the new law requires updated equipment, plan to phase out the old and introduce the new without breaking the bank. You must update your workflows accordingly if there is a procedural change, such as additional reporting requirements. Implementing these updates might involve retraining your staff, which can be as detailed as coaching a sports team on new play tactics. Ensure everyone understands the changes and why they're essential by ensuring that these updates become part of your daily business fabric, not just "another rule" to follow.

Engaging with Legal Professionals

A team of legal professionals can help your business thrive and be more profitable in the long run. For example, hiring a skilled business attorney to be on call can make navigating legislative changes much smoother. They can provide insights into how the changes apply to your business and help craft strategies to ensure compliance. Regular check-ins with your attorney can keep you proactive rather than reactive. Think of them as part of your strategic advisory board, helping you to dodge legal bullets and seize new opportunities created by legislative changes.

Staying informed and compliant with legislative changes is a dynamic and ongoing process. It requires vigilance, quick thinking, and the ability to adapt strategies. By staying informed, assessing impacts, implementing necessary changes, and maintaining solid relationships with legal professionals, you can ensure that your LLC meets its compliance obligations and turns potential challenges into opportunities for growth and innovation. Keep your legal lenses polished and your ears to the ground; the landscape of law and your business are ever-evolving.

11.4 SUCCESSION PLANNING: PREPARING YOUR LLC FOR FUTURE

Succession planning is about ensuring the longevity and continuity of your business, especially when you're ready to retire. It is crucial not just for family-owned firms or partnerships but for any LLC that aims to thrive beyond the tenure of its founders.

Understanding the Importance of Succession Planning

Succession planning is vital for ensuring the continuity and stability of your business. It prepares your LLC for future leadership changes, preventing disruptions that could arise from unexpected departures or retirements. Effective succession planning helps maintain direction and avoids internal conflicts, particularly in family-owned businesses or close partnerships. It also ensures a smooth transition in leadership, safeguarding your business's future success and legacy.

Identifying Potential Successors

Identifying the proper successor is like finding the perfect person for a critical role. You need someone who can keep the business thriving and handle leadership responsibilities. Start by looking within your organization. Identify individuals who demonstrate leadership qualities, share your vision, and bring fresh energy and ideas.

Sometimes, the best candidate might not be from the inside but an external hire who can bring new life into the business. Here, the criteria extend beyond familiarity with the business to strategic vision, industry experience, and a personality fit with your company culture. It's a delicate balance between continuity and innovation. Once you have a shortlist, consider a more formal evaluation process —think leadership assessments or tasking candidates with strategic projects to test their mettle.

Training and Transition Processes

Smooth transitions don't happen overnight. They require structured training processes and a gradual handover of responsibilities. Think of it as a mentorship program where the successor learns the ropes and your business's deep-seated values and quirks.

Set up a timeline for this transition. It could be a few months or even years, depending on the complexity of your business and the readiness of the successor. During this period, involve your successor in decision-making processes, introduce them to key business relationships, and let them lead specific projects or departments. It's like a test drive—it gives them a feel for the driver's seat while you remain in the passenger seat for guidance.

Legal and Financial Considerations

The legalities of transferring ownership can be long and complex. You must revise your operating agreement to reflect the new leadership structure, which might involve changes in ownership shares, voting rights, and member roles. Don't forget the tax implications of transferring ownership. Depending on how your LLC is structured, tax consequences could affect you and the business.

Document all changes thoroughly and ensure they are legally solid to prevent future disputes or liabilities. Consider bringing in your legal and financial advisors to verify everything correctly. This step is crucial for avoiding red tape and ensuring the transition is smooth and free from legal complications.

By carefully selecting and preparing your successor, you ensure your business legacy thrives and adapts, even when you're no longer running your LLC.

The Complete LLC Guide For Beginners

Case Studies and Insights

***

T.J. Griffin

12

REAL-WORLD INSIGHTS AND CASE STUDIES

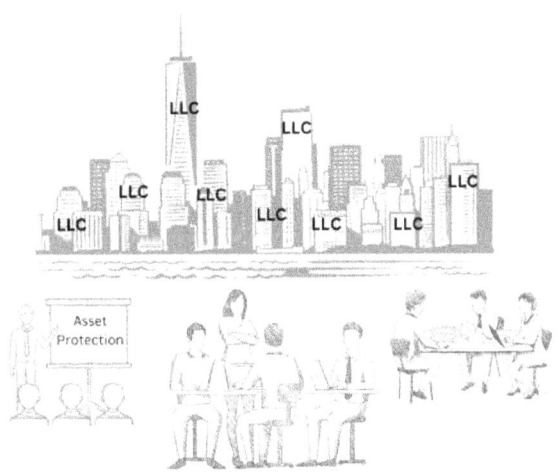

This chapter offers a wealth of real-world wisdom, providing insights from the trenches of LLC ownership. You'll discover how legal strategies work in practice through detailed case studies. Dive into an in-depth look at LLC asset protection, featuring real examples that might inspire you to reconsider your business protection strategy.

12.1 CASE STUDY: SUCCESSFUL ASSET PROTECTION THROUGH AN LLC

Background on the LLC

Imagine a bustling boutique graphic design firm, "Creative Scape LLC," in the heart of a bustling city. The firm started small, a two-person operation that has grown to a team of fifteen over five years. Initially, the significant risk faced was the potential for legal action from clients dissatisfied with copyright infringements, which could spill over and threaten the owners' assets; a classic case where the benefits of an LLC's liability protection could shine, but the owners knew they had to beef up their defenses to safeguard their burgeoning enterprise.

Asset Protection Strategies Implemented

Creative Scape LLC didn't just rely on the default protections of an LLC; they built a fortress. First, the owners separated their high-risk operations by establishing different LLCs for various aspects of their business. Think of it as not putting all your eggs in one basket. For instance, one LLC handled client consultations and contracts, while another controlled copyrighted design licensing. This compartmentalization significantly minimized the risk exposure of each business segment.

Moreover, they invested in robust, comprehensive insurance policies. Opt for business insurance policies specifically tailored to cover the unique risks in graphic design. Ensure you include professional liability insurance, which covers claims of copyright infringement, and general liability insurance, which protects against third-party claims of bodily injury or property damage that could occur during client meetings at your office.

Challenges and Solutions

The road could have been smoother. One major challenge was managing the complexity of operating multiple LLCs. The administrative overhead skyrocketed from separate tax filings to distinct bookkeeping accounts. To navigate these choppy waters, Creative Scape LLC employed a dedicated financial manager whose sole task was ensuring that each LLC's finances were in order, compliant, and transparent. They also invested in an integrated software system that streamlined their operations across the different LLCs, making it easier to manage intercompany transactions.

Another hurdle was ensuring that the insurance coverage matched the evolving scope of their services. As the firm expanded into digital design and online advertising, gaps in its insurance coverage emerged. The solution? Regular insurance audits. Every six months, they sat with their insurance provider to review their policies and adjust coverage as needed, ensuring no new service was unprotected.

Results and Lessons Learned

So, how did these strategies hold up when put to the test? Quite well, actually. When Creative Scape LLC faced a lawsuit alleging copyright infringement by a client competitor, the separate LLC structure prevented the lawsuit from affecting the entire business. The LLC involved handled the legal storm while other business segments remained unaffected. The comprehensive insurance kicked in, covering the legal costs and settlement expenses, thereby protecting the owners' assets and the company's financial health.

From this case study, several key lessons emerge for other LLC owners. First, don't rely on an LLC's inherent protections; actively enhance them based on your business risks. Second, dividing business activities into separate LLCs can be a savvy strategy that requires meticulous financial and operational management. Lastly, regular insurance coverage reviews are crucial as your business evolves. In

LLCs, being proactive about asset protection isn't just brilliant—it's essential for survival.

Now, imagine how you might apply these insights to your own LLC. Whether you're running a high-stakes biotech firm or a cozy local bakery, the principles of risk assessment, strategic protection implementation, and continuous policy review are universally applicable. So take a leaf out of Creative Scape LLC's book; sometimes, a little extra armor is all it takes to turn potential vulnerabilities into fortified strengths.

12.2 FROM STARTUP TO SUCCESS: AN LLC GROWTH STORY

Let's roll out the red carpet for "Green Innovations LLC," a startup that turned the gardening world on its head with eco-friendly, intelligent solutions. A couple of plant enthusiasts, who also happen to be tech geeks, start in a cramped garage with nothing but a big idea and an old laptop. Their initial concept? To revolutionize urban gardening with innovative, space-efficient planters that users could manage via a smartphone app. The startup phase has challenges like limited funding, skepticism from traditional gardeners, and the daunting task of integrating sophisticated technology into something as simple as gardening.

In the early days, "Green Innovations" was all about proving that tech could make gardening accessible and fun. They began with prototype bright planters that allowed users to monitor soil pH, moisture, and nutrient levels through smartphones. However, as cool as the tech was, the early prototypes could have been more varied and user-friendly. It was a classic case of great idea, rough execution. The team spent countless nights in that garage, fueled by pizza and passion, iterating designs until they had a product that was as sleek as it was functional.

As they moved from prototype to production, the founders of "Green Innovations" knew they needed strategies to plant their products in every urban household. Scaling operations was their first move. They transitioned from their DIY garage setup to a small manufacturing facility. This leap allowed for increased production but came with growing pains, such as supply chain management and quality control. They implemented lean manufacturing principles to keep up with these demands and invested in supply chain software that helped streamline operations and reduce waste.

Market expansion was next on their agenda. Initially, "Green Innovations" catered to a niche market of tech-savvy gardeners in urban areas. However, to grow, they branched out by marketing the technological aspects of their products and the environmental benefits. They targeted eco-conscious consumers and partnered with urban sustainability programs, significantly expanding their customer base. Diversification of services also played a crucial role in their expansion strategy. The company ventured into offering full-service urban garden installations and maintenance, which attracted business clients like restaurants and offices wanting to enhance their spaces.

Strategic decisions were pivotal in navigating the company's growth trajectory. One such decision was to pivot their marketing strategy to focus on their products' lifestyle and environmental impact rather than just the technology. This shift appealed to a broader audience and underscored the brand's commitment to sustainability, a core value that resonated strongly with its growing customer base. Another significant decision was to open their API to third-party developers, leading to innovative third-party apps that could interface with their systems, thus enhancing product functionality and user engagement.

The impact of these growth strategies on "Green Innovations" was profound. Financially, the company saw its revenue multiply tenfold in just three years. Market positioning-wise, they were no longer a quirky startup but a leading innovator in urban gardening solutions.

Their growth also had a broader industry influence, prompting traditional gardening supply companies to explore eco-friendly and tech-integrated products. However, with rapid scaling came new challenges, such as managing a larger team, maintaining company culture, and meeting the increased logistical demands. The company had to adapt quickly, prioritizing strategic hires and continuously evolving its operational processes to support its expanded business activities.

"Green Innovations LLC" is a testament to how a simple idea, nurtured with the right strategies and resilience, can grow into a thriving business that generates profit and positively impacts the community and the environment. Their story is an inspiring reminder that with the right mix of innovation, strategy, and grit, the growth possibilities are as limitless as your imagination.

12.3 OVERCOMING COMPLIANCE CHALLENGES: LESSONS FROM AN LLC OWNER

"Hop Innovations LLC," a thriving craft brewery, started making waves for its quirky IPA flavors and rapid expansion into multiple states. As craft beer enthusiasts cheer from various corners, the complexities of adhering to varying state laws about alcohol distribution start to feel less like a mild headache and more like a full-blown hangover. Enter the world of compliance challenges where even a well-intentioned misstep can ferment into a costly legal misadventure.

Initially, Hop Innovations reveled in its grassroots growth, but as it expanded, the patchwork of state regulations became a labyrinth of legalities. Each state had its own set of intricate alcohol distribution laws, some requiring specific labeling, others demanding unique distribution agreements, and a few with stringent advertising restrictions. It was akin to playing a game where the rules differed in every room you entered—exciting yet exasperating.

To navigate these regulatory waters, the brewery took a multi-pronged approach to compliance management. The first was integrating a robust compliance software system tailored to the alcohol industry. This system wasn't just any off-the-shelf software; it was a powerhouse tool that tracked changes in state laws in real-time, ensuring that every batch of beer shipped met the destination state's current legal standards. Think of it as having a GPS that shows the fastest route, alerts you to roadblocks, and reroutes you in real-time.

However, technology alone couldn't brew the perfect compliance strategy. Hop Innovations brought in a team of compliance specialists —legal connoisseurs who understood the nuances of alcohol distribution laws like sommeliers understand grapes. These specialists became the brewery's navigators, advising on everything from label designs to partnership contracts, ensuring each complied with state-specific regulations. They conducted regular compliance training sessions for the team, turning what could be dry legal lectures into engaging, interactive learning experiences that even included compliance trivia contests!

The outcome? Hop Innovations succeeded in maintaining a squeaky-clean legal record as it expanded and built a reputation for reliability and integrity in the craft beer market. Distributors and retailers knew working with Hop Innovations meant fewer legal headaches because compliance was part of the brewery's DNA. This reputation, in turn, opened doors to high-value contracts that smaller or less compliant competitors couldn't access.

From this frothy saga of compliance conquest, several insights bubble up for other LLC owners. One key takeaway is the value of proactive compliance strategies. Waiting for a legal challenge before reviewing your compliance status is like waiting for the roof to leak before checking the weather forecast—ineffective and potentially disastrous. Regularly updating compliance protocols and staying informed about regulatory changes in your industry can prevent many legal storms.

Another lesson is the benefit of viewing compliance as an integral part of business culture, not just a legal necessity. By making compliance a core aspect of operations and involving every employee in compliance practices, businesses can foster an environment where regulatory adherence is as natural as clocking in for the day.

Compliance challenges can seem daunting, especially when crossing state lines or navigating complex industries, but they offer a chance to distinguish your business from the pack. A strong compliance record guards against legal troubles and builds trust with customers and partners, enhancing your business's overall reputation.

So, whether you're crafting beer, building apps, or curating art collections, remember that in the world of LLCs, a stitch in compliance saves nine or perhaps ninety-nine when scaling your business across diverse regulatory landscapes.

12.4 INNOVATIVE FINANCING: HOW AN LLC SECURED NON-TRADITIONAL FUNDING

Imagine trying to navigate the challenging world of funding a startup LLC. Meet "EcoWear LLC," a vibrant startup focused on eco-friendly apparel. They had ambitious dreams and innovative designs, but their limited financial resources needed to be improved. Traditional funding routes like bank loans were difficult to secure due to their youth and unconventional business model centered on sustainability in an industry known for waste.

Financial Challenges

The financial roadblocks for EcoWear LLC were hefty. Banks waved them away due to the lack of collateral and proven market potential, which were deal-breakers. Venture capitalists? Given the unpredictable nature of fashion trends, they were intrigued but hesitant about the return on investment. EcoWear needed cash to kickstart production and get their organic threads on racks but found traditional funding doors slamming shut.

Innovative Funding Solutions

Not ones to be easily discouraged, EcoWear turned its eyes to more creative, somewhat unconventional funding avenues. Crowdfunding became their first port of call. They launched a Kickstarter campaign with catchy videos and heartfelt stories about the impact of sustainable clothing. It wasn't just about opening wallets but about opening minds to a greener wardrobe.

Simultaneously, they explored strategic partnerships. They teamed up with established eco-friendly brands for co-branded products, tapping into their partners' customer bases and splitting the initial production costs. This strategy halved the financial burden and doubled the marketing power.

But the real kicker was tapping into a network of eco-conscious angel investors. These weren't your suit-and-tie investors but individuals passionate about environmental causes and willing to bet on green ideas. EcoWear presented its business at green tech conferences and sustainability summits, pitching its vision of fashion that doesn't cost the Earth.

Implementation and Results

The blend of crowdfunding, strategic partnerships, and angel investing was a cocktail of success. The Kickstarter campaign exceeded its funding goal, bringing in nearly 150% of the target amount. The funds represented more than just money; they symbolized a community of supporters rallying around their cause, preordering products, and spreading the word.

The partnership with established eco-brands brought EcoWear into the mainstream market faster than any traditional marketing blitz could have. It was a credibility booster, a sales accelerator, and a profit-maker all rolled into one.

Angel investors provided not just funds but valuable mentorship. Their expertise in navigating the green market was crucial in refining EcoWear's operations and outreach strategies.

Evaluation and Future Financial Strategy

Looking back, EcoWear's dive into non-traditional funding filled their coffers and expanded their community and market reach. The success of their initial efforts has laid a solid financial runway for future collections and expansions. Now, with a proven track record, even those once-skeptical traditional financiers are starting to show a flicker of interest.

For the road ahead, EcoWear plans to blend traditional and nontraditional funding. They're considering a line of credit from a bank to smooth out cash flow peaks and valleys—a more conventional tool now within their reach, thanks to their proven success. However, the heart of their strategy remains rooted in community-driven, sustainable funding methods. Crowdfunding new collections and nurturing ongoing relationships with their eco-angel investors will continue to fuel their growth, keeping their finances as sustainable as their fashion.

Like EcoWear, stepping off the beaten path can sometimes lead to a river of opportunity. Innovative funding strategies, whether through crowdfunding, partnerships, or finding your tribe of investors, can jumpstart your business and align closely with your brand values and mission.

EMPOWERING YOUR BUSINESS FUTURE

"The best way to predict the future is to create it."

— PETER DRUCKER

With all the tools and knowledge to establish and manage your LLC, it's time to pass on your newfound knowledge and show other readers where they can find the same help.

By leaving your honest opinion of this book on Amazon, you'll show other aspiring entrepreneurs where they can find the information they're looking for and pass on their passion for starting a business. Your feedback will also show others where they can find guidance to navigate the complexities of LLC formation and management.

Simply scan the QR code below to leave your review:

https://www.amazon.com/review/create-review?&asin=B0DMTQFGPM

Thank you in advance for your help. Your contributions help keep the spirit of entrepreneurship alive, empowering others to follow in your footsteps and finally achieve their business dreams.

Here's To Your Success,

T. J. Griffin

CONCLUSION

You now have a comprehensive understanding of "What is an LLC?" from their foundational concepts to the nuances of asset protection and tax strategies. We've covered essential steps for LLC formation, navigated state-specific regulations, and provided insights on financial management and growth strategies.

The world of LLCs is dynamic, with evolving laws, emerging technologies, and shifting market trends. Staying informed and adaptable is vital for your business's success. Consulting with legal, financial, and tax experts will help you navigate challenges.

Armed with this knowledge, you are well-prepared to enter the world of LLC. Every successful business starts small, and you can achieve great things with perseverance and hard work.

It's time to move forward and take the next step:

Register your business name, draft your Articles of Organization, and embark on your entrepreneurial journey. Share your stories and triumphs as you grow. Your journey is just the beginning of an exciting adventure.

CONCLUSION

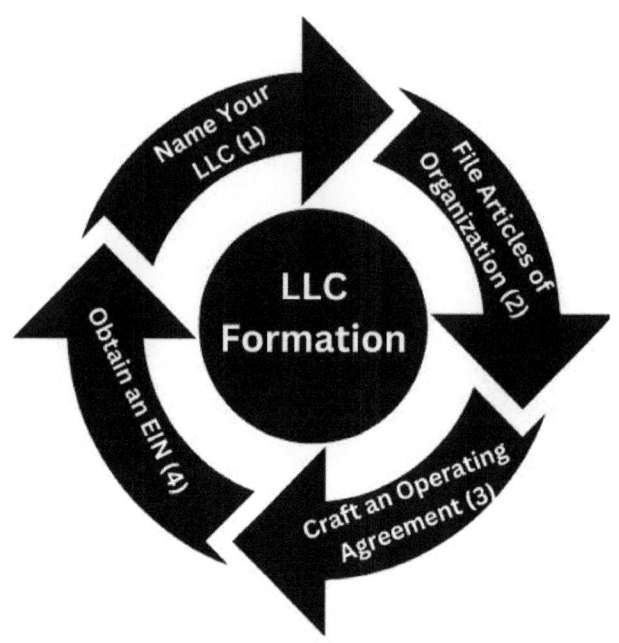

Here's to your success and the prosperous future of your new LLC. May your business thrive, your risks be managed effectively, and your efforts yield rewards. Let's turn your entrepreneurial dreams into reality.

Cheers to you and your new adventure in owning an LLC!

GLOSSARY OF TERMS

Articles of Organization
The document you file with your state to officially form your LLC includes essential information like the LLC's name, address, and members' names.

Limited Liability Company (LLC)
A business structure that offers limited liability protection to its owners (members) while allowing profits and losses to be passed through to their income without facing corporate taxes.

Operating Agreement
An internal document that outlines the LLC's ownership and operating procedures. It includes details on how the LLC will be managed, how profits and losses will be distributed, and how decisions will be made.

Employer Identification Number (EIN)
The IRS assigns a unique nine-digit number to identify your business for tax purposes. This number is necessary for hiring employees, opening business bank accounts, and filing taxes.

Pass-Through Taxation
A tax feature of LLCs where the business's income and losses are reported on the owners' tax returns, avoiding the double taxation corporations face.

Registered Agent
An individual or business entity designated to receive legal documents on behalf of the LLC. This person or entity must be available during regular business hours at a physical address in the state where the LLC is formed.

Franchise Tax
A fee that some states charge LLCs for the privilege of doing business in the state. It's not based on income but rather a flat fee or a percentage of the LLC's revenue.

Sole Proprietorship
A business structure is where one person owns the business and is personally responsible for its debts and liabilities. Unlike an LLC, there is no legal separation between the owner and the company.

Partnership
A business structure where two or more individuals share ownership and are jointly responsible for the business's debts and liabilities. Partnerships can be general or limited, with varying levels of liability and involvement.

Corporation
A business structure that is a separate legal entity from its owners, offering strong liability protection. It is more complex to manage and subject to double taxation, where the corporation pays taxes on its income, and shareholders pay taxes on dividends.

Disregarded Entity
A single-member LLC that is not considered separate from its owner for federal tax purposes. The LLC's income and expenses are reported on the owner's tax return.

S Corporation
A special tax designation that LLCs and corporations can elect, allowing them to pass corporate income, losses, deductions, and credits through to their shareholders for federal tax purposes.

Certificate of Good Standing
A document issued by the state that verifies that an LLC is compliant with state regulations and authorized to conduct business.

Commingling Funds
Mixing personal and business finances can jeopardize the liability protection provided by the LLC structure. Maintaining separate bank accounts and financial records for personal and business expenses is crucial.

Piercing the Corporate Veil
A legal concept where a court disregards the LLC's separate legal status, allowing creditors to pursue the owner's assets if the LLC's formalities are not adequately maintained.

Zoning Laws
Local regulations dictate how property in certain geographic zones can be used. They can affect where you can operate your business and the permitted activities.

General Liability Insurance
A type of insurance that protects your business from claims involving bodily injury, property damage, and personal injury.

Professional Liability Insurance
Also known as Errors and Omissions (E&O) insurance, it covers legal costs and damages resulting from professional services that caused a client financial harm due to mistakes or failure to perform.

Property Insurance
Insurance that covers damage to your business property from events like fire, theft, and natural disasters.

SEP IRA (Simplified Employee Pension Individual Retirement Arrangement)
A retirement savings plan that allows self-employed individuals and small business owners to make contributions toward their own and their employees' retirement savings

Solo 401(k)
A retirement savings plan designed for self-employed individuals with no employees, allowing for higher contribution limits than traditional IRAs.

Doing Business As (DBA)
A registration allows an LLC to operate under a different name from its legal, registered name. This can be useful for branding or marketing purposes.

Statement of Information
Some states require a periodic filing to keep the state updated on an LLC's essential information, such as its address, members, and registered agent.

Personal Property Tax
A tax is imposed on a business's personal property, such as equipment, furniture, and machinery.

Gross Receipts Tax
Some states and localities impose a tax on a business's total revenue rather than on its net income.

Cash Accounting
An accounting method where transactions are recorded when cash is received or paid.

Accrual Accounting
An accounting method where transactions are recorded when they are earned or incurred, regardless of when cash is exchanged.

Nexus
A legal term referring to the sufficient physical presence or connection a business has in a state to be subject to its tax laws.

Foreign Entity
A business registered to operate in a state other than where it was initially formed.

Traditional IRA
A retirement savings plan where contributions are tax-deductible, but withdrawals during retirement are taxed.

Non-Disclosure Agreement (NDA)
A legally binding contract that ensures confidentiality between parties to protect sensitive information.

Utilizing Management Tools
Tools and software used to streamline business operations and improve efficiency.

SOPs (Standard Operating Procedures)
Documented procedures that outline how to perform specific tasks to ensure consistency and quality.

Bootstrapping
Starting and growing a business using personal finances or operating revenue without external funding.

SBA (Small Business Administration)
A U.S. government agency that provides support to small businesses through loans, contracts, and counseling.

Crowdfunding
A method of raising capital by soliciting small amounts of money from a large number of people, typically via the internet.

Reward-Based Crowdfunding
A type of crowdfunding is one in which backers receive a tangible reward or product in return for their contribution.

Equity-Based Crowdfunding
A type of crowdfunding where backers receive shares or equity in the company in return for their investment.

Debt-Based Crowdfunding
A type of crowdfunding where backers lend money to a business with the expectation of being repaid with interest.

ROI: Return on Investment)
A measure of the profitability of an investment is calculated as the net profit divided by the initial cost of the investment.

REFERENCES

- *How to Start an LLC | 8 Easy Steps to Form an LLC - Nolo* https://www.nolo.com/legal-encyclopedia/form-llc-how-to-organize-llc-30287.html
- *Compare S corporation vs. LLC: Differences & benefits* https://www.wolterskluwer.com/en/expert-insights/s-corp-vs-llc-differences-and-benefits
- *Maximizing Asset Protection in an LLC - Bridge Law LLP* https://www.bridgelawllp.com/maximizing-asset-protection-in-an-llc/
- *How the LLC Pass-Through Taxation Works* https://www.nasdaq.com/articles/how-the-llc-pass-through-taxation-works
- *How to choose an LLC name: Tips for naming your LLC* https://www.legalzoom.com/articles/how-to-choose-an-llc-name
- *How to File LLC Articles of Organization:* https://www.nerdwallet.com/article/small-business/articles-organization
- *undefined* undefined
- *Apply for an Employer Identification Number (EIN) online:* https://www.irs.gov/businesses/small-businesses-self-employed/apply-for-an-employer-identification-number-ein-online.
- *Accounting for LLC: Basics, Best Practices & Tax Obligations* https://profitlineusa.com/accounting-for-llc-basics-best-practices-and-tax-obligations/
- *Best Accounting Software For Small Business 2024* https://www.forbes.com/advisor/business/software/best-accounting-software/
- *Maximizing LLC Tax Benefits and Tax Write-Offs - Taxfyle* https://www.taxfyle.com/blog/llc-tax-write-offs
- *How to Build Business Credit for an LLC | Nav* https://www.nav.com/blog/how-to-build-credit-for-an-llc-29964/
- *50-State Guide to Forming an LLC* https://www.nolo.com/legal-encyclopedia/form-llc-in-your-state-31019.html
- *Qualifying to Do Business Outside Your State* https://www.nolo.com/legal-encyclopedia/qualifying-do-business-outside-state-29717.html
- *What you should know about zoning laws* https://www.legalzoom.com/articles/what-you-should-know-about-zoning-laws
- *California vs New York LLC: Which is Better?* https://legal-explanations.com/formation/state/california-vs-new-york/
- *How to protect your assets as an LLC owner* https://www.legalzoom.com/articles/llc-asset-protection-how-to-protect-your-personal-assets-as-an-llc-owner

REFERENCES

- *LLC Insurance: Best Options for Your Business in 2023* https://www.nerdwallet.com/article/small-business/llc-business-insurance
- *undefined* undefined
- *How to protect your assets as an LLC owner* https://www.legalzoom.com/articles/llc-asset-protection-how-to-protect-your-personal-assets-as-an-llc-owner
- *20 Best Business Management Software of 2024* https://peoplemanagingpeople.com/tools/best-business-management-software/
- *Independent contractor (self-employed) or employee?* https://www.irs.gov/businesses/small-businesses-self-employed/independent-contractor-self-employed-or-employee
- *The Ultimate SOP Guide For Small Business Owners* https://medium.com/@kylegillette83/the-ultimate-sop-guide-for-small-business-owners-83ca3ef75607
- *Crisis Management Strategies for Small Business Owners* https://codedesign.org/crisis-management-strategies-small-business-owners-tips-and-tricks
- *14 Customer Retention Strategies That Work In 2024* https://www.forbes.com/advisor/business/customer-retention-strategies/
- *LLC mergers* https://www.thetaxadviser.com/issues/2020/jun/llc-mergers.html
- *5 Digital Marketing Trends To Expect In 2023* https://www.forbes.com/sites/forbesagencycouncil/2023/03/31/5-digital-marketing-trends-to-expect-in-2023/
- *Empowering Small Business: The Impact of Technology on ...* https://www.uschamber.com/small-business/smallbusinesstech
- *State Guide to LLC Report and Tax Filing Requirements* https://www.nolo.com/legal-encyclopedia/50-state-guide-annual-report-tax-filing-requirements-llcs
- *LLC Compliance Checklist* https://www.process.st/templates/llc-compliance-checklist/
- *Small Business Dispute Resolution: A Complete Guide* https://sequoialegal.com/blog/small-business-dispute-resolution
- *It's Important to Keep Your Operating Agreement Updated* https://www.l4sb.com/blog/keep-your-operating-agreement-updated/
- *Bootstrapping - Overview, Stages, and Advantages* https://corporatefinanceinstitute.com/resources/management/bootstrapping/
- *How to Prepare for a Business Loan | CO* https://www.uschamber.com/co/run/business-financing/preparing-for-business-loan
- *How to Pitch Investors: 14 Tips to Get Your Startup Funded* https://finmark.com/how-to-pitch-investors/
- *Six examples of crowdfunding successes and why they worked:* https://uk.indeed.com/career-advice/career-development/examples-of-crowdfunding
- *22 small business tax deductions for your return in 2024* https://www.insureon.com/blog/small-business-tax-deductions

REFERENCES | 153

- *What to do when state tax apportionment rules are unfair* https://www.thetaxadviser.com/issues/2023/aug/multistate-businesses-what-to-do-when-state-tax-apportionment-rules-are-unfair.html
- *2023 Year-End Tax Planning For Business Owners* https://www.mlrpc.com/insights/blog/year-end-tax-planning-for-business-owners/
- *Choosing a tax professional | Internal Revenue Service* https://www.irs.gov/tax-professionals/choosing-a-tax-professional
- *The 5 Biggest Business Trends In 2023 Everyone Must Get Ready For Now* https://www.forbes.com/sites/bernardmarr/2022/10/03/the-5-biggest-business-trends-for-2023/
- *4 Ways To Integrate Technology Into Your Small Business* https://www.forbes.com/sites/forbesbusinesscouncil/2022/08/31/4-ways-to-integrate-technology-into-your-small-business/
- *Stay legally compliant | U.S. Small Business Administration* https://www.sba.gov/business-guide/manage-your-business/stay-legally-compliant
- *Top 10 Best Practices for Succession Planning Make Certain Your "Who's Ready Next" List is Solid* https://www.ajg.com/us/news-and-insights/2018/12/top-10-best-practices-for-succession-planning-make-certain-your-whos-ready-next-list-is-solid/
- *LLC Lawsuit Protection: 8 Case Studies* https://www.ultratrust.com/asset-protection-limited-liability-company-8-case-studies.html
- *Strategies on how to successfully grow your LLC business:* https://www.wolterskluwer.com/en/expert-insights/small-business-growth-strategies-for-your-llc
- *Growing your business can trigger legal compliance risks* https://www.wolterskluwer.com/en/expert-insights/growing-your-business-look-out-for-these-legal-compliance-triggers
- *Collab Capital Case Study* https://innovative.finance/case-studies/collab-capital-case-study/

The Complete LLC Guide For Beginners

Congratulations on completing "The Complete LLC Guide for Beginners!"

You now have the knowledge and tools to *FORM* your entity, *MANAGE* your assets, and *MAXIMIZE* tax benefits with confidence. Even with zero business experience, you've learned how simple and rewarding starting an LLC can be.

As you embark on this exciting journey, remember that each step you take brings you closer to business success.

Here's to your future achievements and prosperous endeavors!

* * *

T.J. Griffin

www.ingramcontent.com/pod-product-compliance
Lightning Source LLC
LaVergne TN
LVHW070742270326
834741LV00062B/1112